# CASHING IN

## HOW TO GET REAL VALUE FROM YOUR LIFELONG LEARNING

SUSAN HUGGINS
PETER SMITH

Kendall Hunt
publishing company

Kendall Hunt
publishing company
www.kendallhunt.com
*Send all inquiries to:*
4050 Westmark Drive
Dubuque, IA 52004-1840



ISBN 978-1-4652-4199-3



Printed in the United States of America
10 9 8 7 6 5 4 3 2 1

# CONTENTS

# ACKNOWLEDGEMENTS

First and foremost, we would like to express our thanks for the opportunity to work on this book. We extend our gratitude to all those that helped and supported us in completing this project; our friends and family who provided encouragement; our editors and reviewers who offered valuable feedback; and our former students who allowed us to use their personal stories as lifelong learning examples.

As lifelong learners ourselves, we appreciate the opportunity to share our experiences, knowledge, insights, and life lessons. The lifelong learning trip isn't a single coherent journey, but rather many small journeys with many influencers along the way. This project is possible because of the many people who have influenced our lives. Lessons learned from those we've met casually, taught as students, worked with closely, and collaborated with to assist other lifelong learners are entwined throughout these chapters. It is our hope that you will pay it forward by sharing your experiences with other adult learners, by continuing to expand, support, and recognize learning that happens outside the traditional classroom.

Finally, we would also like to recognize the extraordinary contributions of experiential learning pioneers such as Dr. Morris Keeton, Dr. Arthur Chickering, and Dr. Malcolm Knowles. Their contributions represent the best of the intellectual thinking and actual practice that undergird our understanding of the importance of assessing experiential learning today. Today's practitioners stand on their shoulders.

# SUSAN R. HUGGINS

Susan Huggins has nearly 20 years of experience in higher education administration and nontraditional learning strategies working with employers and local workforce development boards to develop and implement customized training leading to certificate and degree programs.

Prior to her current position as Portfolio Assessment Director with Kaplan Higher Education Group, Susan was Associate Director in the Center for Lifelong Learning with the American Council on Education (ACE) in Washington, D.C., where she utilized her higher education experience to connect adult learners with corporate training to higher education programs through the College Credit Recommendation Service (CREDIT). Before joining ACE, Susan served as the Director of Military and Government Contract Training at Florida Community College at Jacksonville (now Florida State College), where she managed government and military training programs and delivered degree programs for service members through multiple instructional methods. She has experience developing articulation agreements, developing and implementing programs with the intent of creating a smooth educational path for adults.

Susan is a member of the Council on Standards Development for the International Association for Continuing Education and Training (IACET) and is a member of the ePortfolio Committee for the Postsecondary Electronic Standards Council (PESC). In addition to managing the portfolio development and assessment process at Kaplan University, she also teaches and develops curriculum in the management and business fields. Susan is an adult learner herself, continuing her education as an adult. She earned a Bachelor of Science in Workforce Education from Southern Illinois University and her Master of Arts in Organizational Management from the University of Phoenix. She has also completed post-graduate courses with a focus on higher education leadership at the University of Florida.

# DR. PETER SMITH

Peter Smith has been leading innovation in higher education domestically and internationally for more than 40 years. Founder and first president of two colleges, the Community College of Vermont (1970) and California State University, Monterey Bay (1995), Peter has also served as the Dean of the Graduate School of Education at George Washington University and as the Assistant Director General for Education at UNESCO in Paris, France.

Peter's focus throughout his career has been on adult learners, work readiness, new service delivery models, and new ways to recognize learning wherever and whenever it has occurred. As a member of the founding board of the Council for the Assessment of Experiential Learning (CAEL), Peter has worked throughout his career to help lifelong learners use assessment as a pedagogical tool that actually helps them learn more.

Smith has written dozens of articles and three books – *Your Hidden Credentials: The Value of Learning Outside of College* (1986), *The Quiet Crisis: How Higher Education is Failing America* (Anker, 2004), and *Harnessing America's Wasted Talent: A New Ecology of Learning* (Jossey-Bass, 2010).

As Senior Vice President of Academic Strategies and Development at Kaplan Higher Education Group, Peter has been heavily involved in several innovative developments. They include an online and blended approach to assessing prior experiential learning (KNEXT), a consistent approach to using learning outcomes across the curriculum, and most recently, the development of Qualified, a Career planning and development ecosystem. Peter also served in the Vermont State Senate and as Vermont's Lieutenant Governor before entering the US Congress in 1989. He has served on many boards and Commissions including the National Center for Higher Education Management Systems, The Committee for Economic

Development, the Executive Council of the WICHE Center for Education Technology, the Council of State Government's Advisory board on Higher Education, and the President's Forum.

A graduate of Princeton University, Magna Cum Laude (1968) and the Harvard Graduate School of Education (MAT, 1972; EdD, 1982), Peter's professional interest, career and personal journey have helped him become a conscious, reflective, lifelong learner himself.

# INTRODUCTION

*Cashing In* is the result of a collaboration between the authors, new writing combined with material taken from all three of Dr. Smith's previous books. Dr. Smith owns his first book, *Your Hidden Credentials*, outright. Material created from that publication is noted. His second and third books, *The Quiet Crisis* and *Harnessing America's Wasted Talent* are, however, owned by Jossey-Bass publishers. Where appropriate, direct references from these two books are foot-noted in the text and listed at the end of each chapter. In other cases, however, Dr. Smith has written new language around concepts that were first developed in these two books. A good example would be the issues of "information abundance" and "information scarcity" first introduced in *Harnessing America's Wasted Talent.* In these cases, the footnotes are used to recognize where the concept was first introduced, not to attribute the exact language used.

# CHAPTER 1

## Learning from the Experience of Living

Higher education and career education face a day that, honestly, we never thought would come. It is a day in which

- post-secondary learning achieved outside of college is honored as equal to college-based learning;
- post-secondary *personal learning*, done by individuals on their own, is honored as equal to college-based learning;
- employers admit that most college graduates are not ready to work on day one;
- employers report that behavior and soft intellectual skills are equal to or more important than hard skills in terms of worker effectiveness; and
- more employers are ready to bypass college certificates and degrees as proof of readiness and focus directly on workplace skills and abilities.

Many people who have been so near to, yet so far away from cashing in on the value of what they have learned outside of the traditional educational routes, may well say, "It's about time!" They have been caught in a painful and persistent irony. Our folklore is filled with observations about learning and opportunity, like "live and learn," that suggest learning can happen, and pay off, in many settings other than college. And we have real time stories now that make the same point. Michael Dell, for example, learned how to build a computer not from taking a class, but from taking his computer apart.

# EXPERIENTIAL LEARNING

The point is this: We all know that significant learning occurs outside the university setting. The problem is how to quantify that learning so that future employers recognize its value. Many of us have had the experience of applying for a job with a strong resume of experiences that are overlooked because they are not quantified or formalized in the form of a certification or a degree.

The sad irony is that our higher education institutions do not practice what our cultural mythology preaches. Generally, they have not acknowledged life experience when awarding credit or deciding whether or not a student can "test out" of a class and begin their studies at a higher level. Put another way, there are no standardized exams in subjects like project management or financial planning.

We know, however, that you do learn from the experience of living; that there are strong and useful connections between *effort*, *learning*, and *success.* Most of us learn actively and purposefully, outside of college, on an ongoing basis. As Allen Tough's research in *The Adult's Learning Projects* (1971) reveals, the average person spends more than 700 hours *every year* acquiring new knowledge and skills. For example, you are learning when you

- read about child development and discuss parenting with a friend or a group in order to cope better with the children in your life;
- take a series of courses at work to be certified in a new application process;
- attend a demonstration of a new technique by your supervisor, or attend a workshop run by an outside expert in the industry;
- study and develop a new health and diet plan to keep physically fit;
- take several courses through continuing education;
- engage in therapy;
- research the culture and geography of a foreign country before visiting the country;
- buy a new piece of electronic equipment and spend time learning how to use it; or
- learn to play a new instrument or learn a new sport.

## Characteristics of Experiential Learning

Experiential learning has three important characteristics:

- ***It is personal.*** Learning is shaped to and by your unique-ness. One person is moved to tears upon hearing the story of Lincoln's childhood, whereas another yawns. A young woman, recently orphaned, reads a psychology text in ways that a retired autoworker who has returned to college for a few classes cannot imagine, and the inverse is equally true. One person's revelation about culture and diversity is another's confirmation. We learn as we are, influenced by our hopes and our fears, our faiths and our singular experiences.
- ***It is purposeful.*** Learning happens when we want and need it to. We read and remember the essence of a passage because it explains our lives a little bit, we think the passage shows great insight, and we want to quote it to someone else. We admire a skill or a resource that someone else has, and want to learn it ourselves. We may forget why we first started; we may shift what we value most; but we are, in fact, learning because each of us, as an individual, wants and needs to.

- ***It is powerful.*** Learning, unlike nearly anything else, bears down on us in ways that change us: it revises how we think about things, how we feel, how we behave. It yields new skills with which we can surprise or delight others or ourselves. It enables us to rise above our places in society by showing others our unique, hidden credentials. Even if we are not thinking about what we are doing as learning, checking an old recipe in a worn cookbook, writing and reading a journal, seeing a counselor, it is, in fact, what we are doing.

## History of Experiential Learning

Happily, our capacity to understand the value of experiential learning has increased exponentially since the 1970s. America has generated a new learning ethos, a stunning development in understanding learning that supports the emerging diversity of learning opportunities. Not only have we witnessed a staggering expansion of the number and types of colleges, but we also have seen an equally robust expansion of our knowledge about how we learn. Here are some examples:

- In 1971, Dr. Allen Tough began to define and describe informal learning with his book, *The Adult's Learning Projects: Fresh Approaches to Theory and Practice in Adult Learning*. In this groundbreaking work, Tough "belled the cat," identifying the existence, the amount, and the value of experiential learning. For educators and employers alike, the research changed the ground rules that underlie the relationship between education, training, and readiness to work. Decades later, boosted by the capacity brought by technology, those changes are accelerating.
- A bit more than a decade later, in 1983, Howard Gardner authored *Frames of Mind* in which he began to develop his theory of multiple intelligences that bridge cultural perspectives on human learning. Gardner's work, among other things, offered a new and important perspective on how people learn and, consequently, how they approach problems and challenges at work.
- Similarly, Barry Sheckley and Morris Keeton (2001) advanced the concept of learning retention, the relationship between how something is learned and how long the learner can remember and apply it. This work clarifies the value of experiential and active learning as *stickier* than traditional learning when it comes to retention and application of what was learned.

Although this new and emerging knowledge has informed further research and led to improved practice, the incidence of recognizing and assessing experiential learning has not expanded proportionately. Because traditional collegiate instruction goes on in a *faculty-centric* environment, it has been difficult to implement new, consistent ways of looking at learning and assessment through IT-supported advanced curriculum design. With the arrival of modern technology, and the support it gives to information accessibility and consistency, we have reached a *tipping point* in that now we can provide learners with a supported environment to collect, store, and document their experiential learning.

## Changes in Post-Secondary Learning Outside of Traditional Classrooms

In spite of all this knowledge, nothing significant changed in the practices of higher education until recently. Now, however, there is a tsunami of change embracing the importance and incidence of valuing post-secondary learning that happens outside of college. Why? What has happened? Although this is not the main topic of this book, it is important to understand why this change is not a passing fad or fancy. It is fundamental.

There has been a trifecta of circumstance and events that has taken learning over the threshold into a new world.

**Technology** Improvements in technology have made it possible to make learning opportunities available anytime, anywhere. And as the emergence of Massive Open Online Courses (MOOCs) amply demonstrates, terrific content is readily available at low cost or for free. Place-based education, the campus, becomes an option, not a necessity. An important part of this change is its financial consequence. Technology makes it cheaper and more convenient to research opportunities and do what it takes to get credit for life experience.

**Supply and Demand** In a world of accelerating change in the workplace, there is a growing gap between the number of people with the skills needed for entry into the workforce and the number of jobs requiring those skills. Employers are unable to hire the people they need because colleges are not graduating them in sufficient numbers. This gap between the supply and demand of skilled workers drives the search for and attractiveness of new ways of validating knowledge and skills, like assessing experiential learning.

**Rising Prices** Simultaneously, colleges are experiencing dramatically rising prices. Again, the pressure for lower cost, more effective educational models, including assessment of experiential learning is seen as part of the solution.

## A NEW AGE FOR LEARNING AND ASSESSMENT

We can see that the non-traditional has become the traditional. But why is the assessment of experiential learning more important than ever before? The answer is pretty clear. The proportion of adults 25 and older engaged in higher education is increasing faster than that of traditionally-aged (18- to 24-year old) students. Put another way, the once non-traditional adult enrollment is now the traditional. According to a 2012 report by the U.S. Department of Education, National Center for Education Statistics (NCES), the percentage increase of non-traditional students age 25 and over has been larger than the percentage increase in the number of younger students. Between 2000 and 2010, the enrollment of students under the age of 25 increased by 34 percent while the enrollment of students age 25 and over rose 42 percent. The continued rise in the enrollment of adult learners in higher education is expected to continue. Looking forward from 2010 to 2020, NCES projects an eleven percent increase in enrollments of students under the age of 25 and a 20 percent rise in enrollments of students 25 and over (U.S. Department of Education, 2012). With this increase, the importance of recognizing and assessing experiential learning along with other non-collegiate sources of learning also increases. The shift in *who* is going to college, taken in concert with the shift in *what* they need to learn (the skills gap), creates an economic imperative to speed the adoption of new, high quality practices in assessment as part of the solution. It is no longer simply an *academic* issue.

For the first time in our history, business, labor, political, and (some) educational leaders are calling for an acceptance of learning done outside of college as a way to reduce time and cost to gain a credential, if the learning can be verified as being at the post-secondary level. More specifically, for the first time since the rise of mass public higher education in the 1950s, many employers are eager to know clearly what employees know and can do, regardless of their academic attainment. And institutions such as Western Governors

University, Southern New Hampshire University, Excelsior College, Charter Oaks State College, Kaplan University, and Mount Washington College are employing *direct assessment* of competence, not just courses or time, to chart progress towards the degree.

Be aware, however, that while the assessment of prior experiential learning is more readily available, it is also very difficult work. It requires rigorous reflection on your prior learning, solid evidence of your learning, and a written analysis of knowledge, skills, and ability. It is not an *end run* around traditional coursework. Rather, it is a direct approach to understanding clearly what you know and can do, and what the value of your knowledge is to you, your career, and your future academic record.

## Reflecting on Your Learning

Consider reflection. Reflection, as it pertains to portfolio development and assessment, is a part of the learning process. Chapter Four goes into greater detail about the process of personal reflection and how you will connect the reflection to your learning. The Merriam-Webster Dictionary states that reflection is the act of "considering of some subject matter, idea or purpose." The process of reflection (or considering a specific subject, idea, or purpose) provides us with a process to gain a clearer idea of how we use the learning personally.

In fact, we learn as we live, lurching from one thing to another, rarely achieving our goals on first attempts, and learning as we go. Sometimes we learn as a way of coping with personal crises and changes. In these cases, significant learning comes at untidy times in our lives. In addition to the untidiness, however, most of us haven't learned how to reflect consciously and seriously on the fact of our personal learning, let alone its value and impact on us. So, in many cases, personal learning is lodged in our lives as an iceberg of experience revealing only tiny tips of knowledge. Through active reflection we can convert the raw material of experience to the more refined distillate of knowledge, achieving a finer alignment between our lived experience and our conscious knowledge and understanding. Assessment of prior experiential learning helps learners do just that.

## SUMMARY

You can learn from the experience of living. There are tools and resources to help you measure your learning, whether it has occurred on the job or in the community; at the union hall or in the corporate training center; in the military or at a corporate university; and formally or informally. Much of this experiential learning can be recognized for accurate academic and career reward.

It is truly a new age for learning and assessment. We have written *Cashing In* to provide you with knowledge about the resources, institutions, businesses, and agencies that are committed to helping you get the value you deserve for your knowledge, skills, and abilities. In the chapters that lie ahead, we will analyze barriers, describe and explain the assessment process and its uses, and most importantly, provide connections to active resources from which you can construct the best path for you to take as you "cash in" your prior learning for the value you deserve.

## KEY TERMS

**Experiential Learning.** Learning acquired through experience and reflection, as opposed to formal instruction at a college or university

## REFERENCES


Gardner, H. (1983). *Frames of Mind: The Theory of Multiple Intelligences.* New York, NY: Basic Books.

Reflection [Def. 7]. (n.d.) In *Merriam-Webster Online*, Retrieved June 24, 2013, from http://www.merriam-webster.com/dictionary/reflection.

Sheckley, B.G., & Keeton, M.T. (2001). *Improving employee development: Perspectives from tesearch and practice.* Chicago, IL: Council for Adult and Experiential Learning.

Smith, P. (1986). *Your Hidden Credentials: the Value of Learning Outside of College.* Acropolis Books, Inc.

Smith, P. (2004). *The Quiet Crisis: How Education is Failing America.* pp. 45 - 46, 67-68. Anker Publishing Company, Inc. Bolton, MA.

Smith, P. (2010). *Harnessing American's Wasted Talent: A New Ecology of Learning.* Jossey-Bass. San Francisco, CA. (pp 91 - 94).

Snyder, T.D. & Dillow, S.A. (2012). *Digest of Education Statistics 2011* (NCES 2012-001). National Center for Education Statistics, Institute of Education Sciences, U.S. Department of Education. Washington, DC.

Tough, A. (1971). *The adult's learning projects: A fresh approach to theory and practice in adult learning.* Toronto: OISE.

Weathersby, R. & Tarule, J.M. (1979). Adult development and adult learning styles: The message for non-traditional graduate programs. *Alternative Higher Education.* 4 (1), 11-23.

# CHAPTER 2

## Breaking through Assessment Barriers in Higher Education

Higher education's greatest strength, as it was designed, built, and developed, is the collection of resources that each college and university comprises: libraries, laboratories, and, of course, the faculty. Taken collectively, these resources are everything that a campus represents, with its distinctive purpose, schedule, rhythm, and culture. Ironically, however, the traditional design that was once higher education's greatest strength has become potential barriers for adult learners. Without changes to accommodate the adult learner, the resources that support learning now support the idea of scarcity; the insufficient use of resources.

### PRINCIPLE OF SCARCITY IN HIGHER EDUCATION

Our colleges have traditionally been organized around the principle of scarcity, that the resources needed to provide an education must be collected in one place, a campus, because there is an insufficient supply of those resources in the surrounding community. And, in fact, from the 1500s through 1990, this was largely the case. The principle of scarcity says that for an institution to be useful to the community around it, it must offer a service that community members cannot get more cheaply or with higher quality elsewhere. Scarcity, based on an inability to duplicate the resource, defines the market. And scarcity was the reality in the world of information, teaching, and learning until the early 1990s when the Web was born. Before technology revolutionized the landscape, there was simply no other way to "do" higher education. The campus was an oasis in an information desert.

## Scarcity of Access

Information and resource scarcity drove *access scarcity* as well. There were only so many slots in each college that were open for students to occupy. As a result, access to college traditionally favored people who had time for college, could afford college, and could learn effectively at colleges as they were structured.

Scarcity, and the academic policies that came with it, created a standard for access that favored some students over others. Among the "others" were adult learners who learned differently, had to work, or were constrained by other social and economic forces. For years, such incentives as student financial aid were provided to generate greater access for those who had been marginalized financially. But there was no parallel accommodation for people who were marginalized because of other factors, like scheduling and learning style.

As a result, college is still, too often, a series of frustrations for the returning adult learner. Some of the frustrations are petty, but very real:

- The bookstore closes at 4:30 p.m. and you can't get there until 5:00 p.m.
- Your academic advisor doesn't have evening hours and you work during the day.
- The library has only limited hours on the weekends when you can study.
- Many of the courses you need are scheduled at times when you cannot attend.
- Continuing education courses are offered at night, but they are not part of the regular degree program, so their credit does not count.

Other policies are demeaning, if not downright damaging to the adult learner:

- Regardless of what you already know, you find yourself sitting between two recent high school graduates in front of a teacher who is lecturing about something you have already learned on the job.
- Smart high school graduates get valuable college credit and place into higher level courses if they can score well on tests, but there is no way for you to get advanced standing in your areas of work experience and personal learning.
- There is enough financial aid for qualified full-time students, but it seems much harder to get what you need if you are part-time.

The combined message is clear: colleges with policies like these are not designed for today's adult learner.

## Other Points of Scarcity

These and many other individual barriers add up to a giant problem that makes life for the returning adult learner somewhere between frustrating and impossible. But the loss of the knowledge and skills that adult learners already have to offer colleges is perhaps the greatest loss of all. It is financially damaging in that adults have to pay tuition for courses that cover material they already know. It is time-consuming in that it requires adult learners to spend more time earning the certificate or degree that they are pursuing. And it depresses motivation by denying the adult learner the recognition of capacity that they already possess. Better and more comprehensive assessment of the knowledge and skills that adults bring with them to college helps solve this problem. We need to embrace and authenticate learning regardless of where or how it occurred, not pretend that it is inferior. This chapter includes a discussion of several of the barriers that adult learners must break through and describes how they can be overcome.

As you consider the points and stories below and reflect on experiences from your own life or stories from the lives of people you know, you will begin to more clearly see the many barriers to traditional higher education that conspire to keep certain populations, adults in particular, on the outside looking in.

**Psychologically Remote** Colleges tend to be psychologically remote. Scarcity can also lead to an "us vs. them" mindset between those within and outside of a college setting. (In college towns, division between "town and gown" is a similar and overlapping phenomenon.) This mentality is intimidating and potentially damaging to students who try to cross the line. On the one hand, these students feel that they are not worthy of the institution because they are older. They have the feeling that others view them as failures as if they were teenagers being held back in high school. On the other hand, these students know that they are not failures who have been held back and are frustrated because the knowledge and skills that they do bring to the table are not recognized.

In addition to the rules and policies that are unfriendly to adult learners and their talents, another perverse effect of scarcity is that it can diminish or crush hope itself. Listen to Bob as he describes his emotional reaction when he finally went to college. Colleges hold people like Bob at arm's length with a reputation that suggests, "whoever we are here for, we are not here for you." Despite Bob's life experience, he is treated exactly like the 20-year-old sitting beside him. For Bob, in the beginning anyway, college had the aura and the mystery of forbidden fruit. He was sure he would be "dumb" in school.

> *So, I finally dragged myself over to the community college and took two courses. And I was scared to death. I had been at war, in police riots, and a firefighter and that was alright. But now I am going to this college and I am scared to death. I literally had stomach cramps – got physically ill. I really don't know why I was scared. I had no idea . . . no reason . . . it had nothing to do with anything . . . there was no consequence to pay. There was no overt, physical, explicit consequence. I could have gone there, flunked out, and I still would have been a lieutenant in the fire department. Nothing would have changed.*
>
> *I was sold this bill of goods about college, that everyone who graduated from college was far superior to the average guy walking the street. I don't say it's a conspiracy, but I think at some level people actually peddle that attitude to keep some people out of colleges and others in them. Where I come from, it's meant to keep them out.*

**Academically Remote** Colleges can be experientially and academically remote. In far too many cases, as in Alan's case below, colleges don't recognize the value of learning that happens somewhere else, outside of a higher education institution. One of the likely reasons you are reading *Cashing In* is because you do not want the learning that is contained in your entire life experience, work, personal, and social, to go unrecognized and be ignored by arbitrary, outdated, and unnecessary practices. You want to convert your experiential learning to practical and academic value. You also, in all likelihood, want to convert credits earned in other colleges, as well as training you completed in the military, workplace, or the union hall into academic credits that count toward your degree.

> *I have been running my own business for the last ten years. During that time, I have acquired numerous skills and a tremendous amount of knowledge. I am now at that point in my life where I want to move on to the next challenge. Unfortunately, any job listing that I come across that I am qualified for in regard to the position, I do not meet the educational requirements. I know that a degree will open more doors for me. But as I have looked into going back to school, I find that it is an incredibly cumbersome and lengthy process. In many cases, it is simply not doable, especially for a working adult with a family. Instead of discouraging people like me, why don't they embrace us and discover the talent and innovation we can bring to the workforce.*

**Financially Remote** Colleges are, in many cases, financially remote. When they refuse to grant credit for your life experience or refuse to accept credits earned elsewhere, colleges are costing you not just money, but also time. This impact, when coupled with soaring tuition and flat-lined financial aid, is especially pernicious for adult learners. Because adult learners primarily qualify for federal loans, they often opt to self-pay, avoiding increased debt – making credit for prior learning a financial necessity.

**Pedagogically Remote** Colleges can be pedagogically remote. Instead of fitting their teaching to your best learning style, colleges traditionally have "the way we do it here," a one size fits all approach that frustrates many, limiting their learning, and defeats many others outright. For example, while the ability to work on a team might be a highly desirable trait in the workplace, in many colleges teamwork is discouraged because it muddies the ability of the faculty member to "grade the work," to decide which learner did which part of the project. And in a world where guided independent study is a definite pedagogical option, colleges still organize classes and lectures supplemented by textbooks as the dominant approach to teaching and learning. There are at least two problems with holding to the traditional approach. First, most adults are used to hands-on learning—learning through experience and interaction with others. For them, the thought of going back to "being talked at" is not appealing. Second, adult learners tend to be highly practical. They want to focus hard on their short- and long-term goals.

**Organizationally Remote** Colleges are, in too many cases, organizationally remote, even if they are near you. The traditional college schedule rarely aligns well with the other demands on a working adult's life. Between working full-time and family commitments, getting to a campus for classes can often be near impossible. Consider the example of Ed. He is like many adult learners; the lack of a degree caused him to miss job advancement opportunities. Although he had the professional experience, because he didn't have a degree, he wasn't eligible for advancement.

> *That college is right down the road from where I work. I drive past it every morning on my way in and every night on my way out. And yet it might as well be a million miles away! There's no way I can attend classes there and maintain my work and family responsibilities. That's no 'shining city on a hill,' that's effectively a castle with the drawbridge pulled up. Where else can I turn?*

# NEW OPPORTUNITIES: BREAKING THROUGH THE BARRIERS

The previous sections illustrate the variety of problems and the struggles that adults have traditionally faced when trying to return to college. Until recently, there was no alternative to the traditional campus-based higher education model. Fortunately, things are changing, and changing fast. The higher education world has begun to recognize the value of the adult learners. It is using new tools and knowledge to change the rules, reinvent itself, and treat adult learners in vastly more responsive, respectful, and friendly ways.

Three powerful changes are driven by technology: unlimited content, unlimited assessment and credit portability, and mass personalization and customization. Together, they eliminate higher education's culture of scarcity, creating a new ecology of learning.

## Unlimited Content

Public libraries and museums have been referred to as the "universities of the common man." Now, in a startling and equally revolutionary extension of that vision, you can get what you want, when you want it, for your own personal learning and pleasure. Learning is at your fingertips, customized with search engines for the needs or interests that you have.

We have entered an era in which high quality, organized curricula are at the fingertips of every potential learner with Internet access. Students can easily access courses with Open Educational Resources (OER) and Massive Open Online Courses (MOOCs). Then there's the establishment of content providers like iTunesU, Khan Academy, and the Open CourseWare Consortium. Resources like these are available free to anyone, anytime, regardless of whether they are affiliated with a college or not.

In his breakthrough book *The Long Tail* (2006), Chris Anderson provides an explanation for this previously implicit but powerful aspect of the Web. Using the music and publishing industries as examples, Anderson identifies the low cost of storing information once it is on the Web as well as its mobility as the drivers of a world in which any person can get any piece of information at any time for a very low cost

Higher education's "long tail" does the same thing for curricular content. We are entering an age in which more people have access to a previously unimaginable variety of information resources at a fraction of the former price. With the explosive growth of resources like iTunesU, more people, including those who were previously excluded from higher education, will be able to access the exact information they want, when they want.

## Improved Prior Learning Assessment and Credit Portability

For years, we have lived with the knowledge that the barriers to higher education come in many forms, beyond simply getting to a college campus at the right time for a class. But today, the size of the student body does not have to be controlled by available classroom space, faculty, or other resources that are available in a campus setting. Nor do students themselves have to suffer with other limitations that have traditionally come with the campus setting, including colleges' unwillingness to recognize the learning that adults bring with them as a foundation for further learning. There has been a positive shift in the willingness to recognize experiential learning, and many schools, school districts, and even states are putting policies into place to recognize and process non-traditional learning.

In addition, independent third-party evaluators of prior learning have evolved outside of the colleges. Organizations such as KNEXT (www.knext.com) and CAEL's Learning Counts (www.learningcounts.org) allow schools without a formal process to recognize prior learning and outsource prior learning assessment. (See Chapter 3 for more information on prior learning assessment.) This simplifies the process of compiling and submitting a portfolio, enabling the process to be scalable such that thousands of people can participate instead of dozens. More details on preparing a portfolio can be found in Chapter 8.

Today's learners are more mobile than ever, often attending more than one school to earn their degree. It is one thing for people to become increasingly mobile, to be able to learn anything, anytime, anyplace. It is quite another thing, however, to create binding and transparent agreements for the transfer of credit for learning. With mobility increasing, the demands for credit portability at full value will also increase dramatically. Government leaders decry policies and practices that lead to increased spending for redundant services, and employers are becoming increasingly dissatisfied with traditional college transcripts and the resumes to which they contribute, because neither accurately communicates the individual's true capacity. An increasing number of colleges are connecting their learning outcomes to academic policies, program requirements, and workplace requirements to create workplace-college articulation agreements that operate transparently. Learners use these agreements and equivalency measures to move their assessments and the courses wherever and whenever they need to.

## Mass Personalization and Customization

Another barrier to higher education has been the *one size fits all* approach to curriculum design, learning environments, and instruction. But emerging technologies and Web 2.0+ have permanently changed the possibilities and potential of higher education. For example, whereas it was once the case that a visual or kinesthetic learner had to toil through an un-engaging, if not incomprehensible, textbook to try to learn, these students now have access to courses with multimedia and interactive content that plays to their learning styles. Now you have a legitimate right to expect that a college will listen to your story; understand the value of your knowledge, skills, and abilities; and offer a pathway that responds to your expressed needs. Personalization and customization will become part of the routine, not the exception.

**Personalization** Personalization happens when we connect the entire process of education to the life of the learner. We know now that learning happens naturally and continuously, occurring when there is a strong connection between the *it* of whatever is to be learned and the *me* of the lived experience of the learner. The more personally connected the learner is to his or her learning program, the greater the likelihood of success. The less that a formal learning program engages each learner's experience, interest, aspirations, and culture, the less likely it is that the necessary human connections will be made. One hundred years ago, John Dewey, the great education philosopher, made the same point in *Democracy and Education* (1916) that is supported today though the recognition of prior learning. He imagined a synergy between the experience of living and more formal, organized education. And he argued that schools organized around that purpose could successfully incorporate the learning experience of every learner.

As a practical matter, however, Dewey's philosophy and the practices that it suggested did not take root in schools and colleges because information scarcity encouraged a "teacher-centric" model--the traditional, uniform instructional model. Now, however, using assessment of prior experiential learning and other developmental assessments, yesterday's philosophy is today's practical reality.

**Customization** Customization is the process through which the learning experience is adapted to the needs of the learner. Customization involves collecting diagnostic and developmental information for each learner. Accurate data will help all involved adapt your learning program to your needs. The day has come when good diagnostic information can be seamlessly integrated into the learning plans and the pedagogy, aiding teacher and learner alike.

## SUMMARY

At the heart of the matter, there is only one person for whom learning, education, and life happens up close and personal, and that is the learner. Each of us is a personal learner, the conductor of a private symphony, an artist with a private canvas. One of the great gifts that emerging technology gives us is the ability to personalize learning to each learner's interests, strengths, and needs. Personalization begins with assessment of what a learner already knows. The exercises and tools contained in this book, will give the returning adult learners a leg up by helping them learn more about learning assessments that promote seamless transitions between life, work, and degree programs; providing information about colleges with consistent outcomes-based curricula, assessments, and course design; and providing information about colleges that honor the need for portability of earned credit.

Prior learning assessment (PLA), with all of its aspects, cuts across the traditional barriers to higher education, giving you, the adult learner, a gateway to success:

- By recognizing the value in the formal and informal learning you have accomplished previously, Prior learning assessment brings you into the academic equation personally, thus reducing *psychological remoteness.*
- *Experiential and academic remoteness* is dramatically reduced by granting credit for what you already know.
- Prior learning assessment reduces the cost, hence the *financial burden of college*, by reducing time to degree.
- By recognizing learning that has been accomplished in other places and by other means, prior learning assessment reduces *instructional remoteness.*
- And the ability to do all of this online, anytime, anywhere, destroys the *physical remoteness* traditional colleges.

The era of scarcity in higher education is finished, over, done. Traditional colleges are now surrounded by information abundance that they cannot control, and traditionally-organized institutions are no longer the only source of solutions. Scarcity is supplanted by abundance. And abundance gives us the tools to overcome traditional barriers to higher education, including assessment of learning.

We all remember the story in *The Wizard of Oz* where the Wizard gave the Scarecrow his brains. What we tend to forget is that, throughout the story, the Scarecrow has, in fact, a whole bunch of good ideas when the group is faced with obstacles. But the Scarecrow believes he doesn't have brains.

The Wizard assures him that he doesn't need them:

> *"You are learning something every day. A baby has brains, but it doesn't know much. Experience is the only thing that brings knowledge, and the longer you are on earth, the more experience you are sure to get." Still, the Scarecrow insists. The wizard recognizes the scarecrow's dilemma. Although he has experience, the Scarecrow does not have a diploma: "Back where I come from, we have universities, seats of great learning, where men go to become great thinkers. And when they come out, they think deep thoughts, and with no more brains than you have. But they have one thing you haven't got, a diploma." Instead of giving the Scarecrow a brain, he instead confers on him a degree of Doctor of Thinkology.*

Ridiculous? Of course it is. Today, however, the Wizard could get the Scarecrow what he needed without the tomfoolery. In the era of resource abundance and the access it provides, the Scarecrow could cash in his experience for academic credit and be on his way to a degree.

## WEB RESOURCES

### OER Commons

www.oercommons.org

OER Commons is an open network of tools, resources, and curriculum that is free and open.

### iTunesU

http://www.apple.com/education/itunes-u/

Apple in Education: Colleges and universities utilize the iTunes platform to deliver coursework.

### Open CourseWare Consortium

http://www.ocwconsortium.org

An OpenCourseWare (OCW) is a free and open digital publication of high quality college and university level educational materials. These materials are organized as courses, and often include course planning materials and evaluation tools as well as thematic content. OpenCourseWare are free and openly licensed, accessible to anyone, anytime via the internet.

### KNEXT.com

www.knext.com

Through the use of technology and a fully-integrated approach, the Learning Recognition Program helps higher education institutions build or enhance their prior learning assessment offerings and online portfolio management.

**Learning Counts**
www.learningcounts.org
Learning Counts helps you create a learning portfolio to demonstrate your expertise for undergraduate college credit.

## Key Terms

**Prior Learning Assessment (PLA).** Methods of earning college credit for experiential learning (learning acquired outside a traditional classroom; methods include exam and portfolio development

## REFERENCES


Anderson, C. (2006). *The Long Tail: Why the Future of Business is Selling Less of More.* New York, NY: Hyperion.

Dewey, J. (1916). *Democracy and Education.* New York, NY: The MacMillan Company.

LeRoy, M. (Producer), & Fleming, V. (Director). (1939). *The Wizard of Oz* [Motion picture]. USA: Metro-Goldwyn-Mayer (MGM).

Smith, P. (1986). *Your Hidden Credentials: the Value of Learning Outside of College.* Acropolis Books, Inc. (pp 74 - 75).

Smith, P. (2010). *Harnessing American's Wasted Talent: A New Ecology of Learning.* Jossey-Bass. San Francisco, CA (pp 14-15, 67, 95-96, 102, 135-136).

# CHAPTER 3

## Earning Credit for Non-Traditional Learning: Three Personal Perspectives

Prior learning assessment, also known as PLA, is a term that many colleges and universities use to describe the process of earning college credit for the learning that a person has acquired through work and life experience. The goal of PLA is to help adult learners achieve their educational goals and earn college credit for what they already know. PLA not only helps adult learners accomplish the educational goals they set for themselves, but it can also provide a means for them to engage in more advanced coursework more quickly.

For example, let's say you've owned and operated a small business for the past 20 years, and you want to pursue a Bachelor of Business Administration. With the experience you have under your belt, you have likely gained quite a bit of business knowledge, skills, and abilities. Having acquired knowledge in the business field, you probably don't want to take courses focused on the knowledge that you already have. You may even feel as if you could teach the courses yourself! PLA is a valid way of earning college credit for this knowledge so you can move forward with your degree by taking courses that will challenge you to learn new information, rather than just taking up your time with courses that will be strictly review.

# PRIOR LEARNING ASSESSMENT

Prior learning assessment (PLA) is the umbrella term that many colleges and universities use to describe the process by which college credit is awarded for the learning that a person has acquired through work and life experience. PLA is particularly useful for those who have been in the workplace for five or more years. There is no one single method of PLA. PLA actually comprises several well-established, validated, and nationally recognized processes that encompass multiple types of assessments.

Although PLA is attracting more attention, it is not a new idea. PLA has been used to recognize learning acquired outside the traditional classroom since the mid-1940s when the American Council on Education (ACE) began reviewing formal military courses and occupations for returning World War II veterans. Organizations such as ACE, the Council for Adult and Experiential Learning (CAEL), and the College Board have helped bring national attention to the recognition of college-level learning acquired outside the traditional classroom. In 1974, CAEL developed the Standards for Assessing Prior Learning. CAEL's standards continue to be used today by many colleges and universities.

## Recognized and Accepted Methods of Prior Learning Assessment

There are a number of recognized methods of prior learning assessment, and you can expect to pursue credit for prior learning via one or more of the following. (You can find links to more information in the Web Resources section at the end of this chapter.)

**Standardized Exams** Standardized exams such as the College-Level Examination Program (CLEP), Defense Services Standardized Test (DSST), and Excelsior College® Examinations (ECE) help adult learners earn college credit for what they know. These exams are widely recognized and accepted by colleges and universities.

**Challenge Exams** Challenge exams are a quick, economical way to earn college credit for learning acquired outside the classroom. Challenge exams are typically institution-specific and degree-specific. Most challenge exams are developed by a specific program at a school. If you can't find a list of your school's challenge exams, be sure to ask. The exams provide you with an opportunity to assess college-level knowledge through a subject-related exam. You may find that a challenge exam exists for a subject that no standardized exams cover.

**ACE Credit Recommendations** The American Council on Education (ACE) provides adult learners with college credit recommendation for corporate learning. The American Council on Education (ACE) CREDIT Recommendation Service lists all reviewed training in the National Guide to College Credit for Workforce Training. You should check the National Guide for any previous organizations where you have worked that may have had their training reviewed. Training organizations such as the Federal Aviation Administration (FAA) Academy, McDonald's Corporation, and Microsoft Corporation have a lengthy list of training courses that have been reviewed. If you have taken any of the training courses at an organization listed in the National Guide, request for an ACE transcript to be sent to your college along with your college transcripts. The ACE transcripts will be evaluated as transfer credit. Due to increased usage and demand, the reviewed courses have expanded to more than 35,000.

**ACE Military Guide** The ACE Military Guide provides an extensive list of more than 18,000 exhibits of military training and occupations that have a college-level credit recommendation. If you have served in any of the military services, the first step is to obtain your service-specific transcript. The military transcript will list all credit recommendations from completed courses and experience. In addition, the transcript also includes college-level test scores, SOC codes, and academic institution information.

**Portfolio Development and Assessment** Colleges and universities use portfolio development and assessment as a way for adult learners to earn college credit for non-traditional learning. The learning portfolio requires time to thoroughly document the learning you have acquired (see Chapter 4 for more detail). If you have learning that cannot be easily assessed by any other method, portfolio development is certainly an option you should consider. Excellent resources for this assessment are KNEXT (www.KNEXT.com) and Learning Counts (www.LearningCounts.com).

## THE VALUE OF PRIOR LEARNING ASSESSMENT

As an adult, you go back to school with specific needs, needs that have been determined by the workplace, by your experience, and by your personal and professional goals. The challenge, then, is to establish relevance with education programs that are more responsive to your needs, more respectful of your capabilities, and more integrated with the workplace.

At the heart of PLA is the idea that every person has derived value from his or her experience that can be validated in terms that are widely accepted, much the same way that classroom learning is validated by grades and credits are represented on transcripts. Validation of prior learning requires a standard approach for documenting and assessing your learning.

As the following three stories will attest, there are other extraordinary values that are unearthed by the portfolio development process. Learner after learner reports discovering significant added value in his or her life history after going through a PLA process. Learners report significantly changed self-images and very different views of learning and education than they held before going through the PLA process. And they indicate that, in fact, life experience can be a tremendous asset to their future personal as well as professional growth.

### First, Meet Martha

Martha is a divorced housewife who was forced to return to work and school at age 38. With only a high school diploma, Martha felt that it was important to complete a bachelor's degree. She decided to get a jump on the degree by pursuing PLA in topics she felt she had significant experience, in particular, child psychology. As Martha looked back over her experience as a housewife and mother, she showed confidence in the decision to continue her education. Much to her surprise, however, her portfolio preparation experience did more than earn her some college credit. It also taught her more about learning, knowledge, and how society works than she ever expected to pick up in any classroom.

*Learning is a matter of survival. And, it is important to know the value of what you have learned. [Prior learning assessment] helped me learn that I had done an awful lot in my life that I just didn't really think amounted to anything or served any particular purpose. It had never been put to me that the things I had done were of value. It was just taken for granted that you did them.*

*Here I was, uneducated with only a high school degree, but I certainly did a lot of child psychology raising four kids. I was actually doing the child psychology without reading up on it. I wasn't knowledgeable as far as having a degree in it. But through experience and hit and miss, I found out which things worked and which things didn't. Maybe I didn't know what the great philosophers thought, but I certainly knew that you handled one child in one manner and another in an entirely different manner.*

*Those who have not had a college education, we did it the hard way, learning by the mistakes we made and by the mistakes of our friends and parents. Now, these same mistakes that we learned by doing are the examples they use in the books they teach us from. When you look at it that way, it is even funnier. It's all basically the same knowledge; it's just that there is a formal way of learning it and an informal way of learning it. I think it is better to have the experience first, kind of like a lab. You can understand it and cope with it and kind of relive it when you go to school. Then you say, "By golly, that's right! It really does work that way." But, if you haven't had the experience, you can only assume it works that way because you don't have first-hand knowledge.*

*When I finally thought about what I had learned, things that I thought were insignificant all my life became important. I had seen them just as a matter of life, yet they were knowledge. Seeing and understanding that knowledge from your life is a great tool for even more learning that many people don't pay attention to.*

*The question is, "What do you want to do with the knowledge?" You wouldn't want to get a college degree just to say that you had one. You don't need a degree to get more knowledge. You can go to any library and pick up a zillion books, or conduct searches on the Internet, and learn that way if that's what you want to do. But the degree is of value to you. It is a tangible thing that you can actually show people and say, "Look, I have accomplished this much and now I can go further from here."*

## Peg's Story

Meet Peg. Peg had two asthmatic children and she wanted better health care services for them in the community. After attending a meeting on community health care issues, she became deeply involved in a new community health care initiative. Within a year, and with only a high school diploma, Peg was the director of a new health center. It was then that Peg decided to pursue a college degree.

Peg describes what it is like to go to college, and the value of developing her portfolio as an early step towards completion. Just like Martha, what Peg learned in the process of getting her degree included more than the content. She discovered that her real life experience added value and context to the school-based learning she used to complete her degree.

*One day, I heard there was a meeting around health care issues in my community and I decided to go. I became very interested in these issues. Eventually the group asked me to chair those meetings. I knew absolutely nothing about chairing meetings. I didn't know protocol. But I did it. After working just over a year, we were able to open the doors of the center.*

*Then, the board asked me to take on the job as director of the center. I was very uncomfortable with that because I was concerned that I wouldn't do the community just service because I had no education. But I knew what the community would accept and what they would not. I also knew my limitations and wasn't afraid to ask for help.*

*I didn't know what the future was going to bring and I saw this as an opportunity to do something about it for myself. For example, if, for some reason, I decided to leave the health center, maybe I wouldn't even be talked to by other groups because I didn't have the piece of paper.*

*The actual deciding factor in going [back to school] was that I learned about a program that allowed me to use some of the things that I've already accomplished towards the degree. So, it wouldn't take that long or cost as much because I wouldn't be repeating things I already knew. So, I didn't have to go the route of a four-year program with four courses a semester to earn the degree. I didn't have the time, the patience, or the inclination to do that.*

*I found it to be a tremendously exciting experience – I liked it very much. It was very difficult to hold down a full-time job, go to school, take care of a family, and do it all in 15 months. Even then, though, in the beginning I was not sure what the degree was going to teach me. Not that I think I know it all and can't learn. I learn every day of my life. But what are they going to teach me that I could benefit from on this job?*

*I see so many people coming out of school with a degree in their hand and, quite frankly, they don't know what to do with it. They've learned in the books, but it's not the real work. Let's take "determination of need," for example. The book says you fill out an application like this and file it over there and then you take it here and there – through the process – that's what you learn in school. The real world is that the piece of paper is only a small part of it. Like, that piece of paper is a waste of time because nobody ever reads it. They turn around and ask you ten times the same 80 questions. You have to depend on the personalities of the people you go before in the process. That's the real world...the roadblocks, the setbacks.*

## And Now, Phil's Story

Phil had all the traditional reasons for finishing his degree—better job opportunities and personal satisfaction being primary among them. But what he didn't know, and couldn't have imagined, was the personal impact that completing a portfolio would have on him. At first, he was simply astonished at what he *knew*: things that he had forgotten before he began sifting through his life experiences as we describe in Chapter 4 But then his growth extended and deepened as he became ever more self-reflective about his management style and workplace responsibilities.

*My boss was talking about retiring and I wanted to sit in his chair. His job description required a baccalaureate and I only had an associate degree. Since I got the [associate] degree, I've spent all my time taking classes that were convenient: one-week seminars and one-day work shops. I've accumulated all this time and experience and never got any credit for it.*

*With the age of my children and their activities, going back to school was just too much of a problem. I knew how hard I worked just to get the associate degree. Now I'm at the point of saying, "Hey, I need the paper, but more important, I want the satisfaction of saying that I've got the college degree."*

*Then I found a college that would consider giving me credit for learning I had done outside of school. So I looked into it and saw what was available. The program made a big difference for me beyond getting the credit. As I got more into the program, I found out that I knew more than I thought I did. I started listing all the things I had done in my life, and I suddenly realized that I had done a lot more than I thought I had. The writing helped me remember and it brought my learning all back up to the surface. I think we lose knowledge because we aren't challenged to use it. Much of what I know is in the back of my mind. It just needed to surface.*

*I did a paper on planning that had to do with project management and managing by objectives. I got looking at it, reading up a little on project and critical-path management. These were things I had been doing for years, but I never put a label on it. The assessment program is all about what you have learned away from school. It's not what you have done, or experienced, but what you learned as a result. That's the important part.*

*I saw the difference between something I did and how I changed as a result. I thought about how I used to react to a certain type of supervision from my boss when I started work. Then, when I became a supervisor, I observed others' management styles and how I reacted to the task. I was able to see a change in myself. I could say, "Hey, I can see where I went from being this type of manager to being this type." Or, I could see where I started thinking about my responsibilities as a manager rather than just being a manager. I realized what it really meant and what I had to do.*

## SUMMARY

From these three stories, you can see first-hand how the portfolio development process, done rigorously, yields extraordinary learning *in addition to* the learning that is awarded credit. Aspirations lift. Capacity to learn and do is reinforced and strengthened. Confidence increases. And academic/career focus clarifies and strengthens, improving performance after the course or program is completed.

As previously mentioned, prior learning assessment is not new. It has been used to recognize learning acquired outside the traditional classroom since the mid-1940s. The goal of PLA is to help adult learners achieve their educational goals and earn college credit for what they already know. PLA not only helps adult learners accomplish the educational goals they set for themselves, but it can also provide a means to engage in advanced coursework more quickly, saving valuable time and money. Furthermore, it provides learners an opportunity to reflect on and recall what they have already learned, allowing them to more effectively build upon their prior learning and integrate it into their future studies and work.

## Key Terms

**Portfolio.** A collection of evidence that supports a learner's claim for credit

**Prior Learning Assessment.** Methods of earning college credit for experiential learning (learning acquired outside a traditional classroom; methods include exam and portfolio development

## WEB RESOURCES

You may wish to consult the following resources for more information about prior learning assessment.

### ACE National Guide to College Credit for Workforce Training

www.acenet.edu/nationalguide

The American Council on Education's ACE National Guide to College Credit for Workforce Training contains ACE credit recommendations for formal courses or examinations offered by various organizations, from businesses and unions to the government and military.

### ACE Guide to the Evaluation of Educational Experiences in the Armed Services

http://www.acenet.edu/news-room/Pages/Military-Guide-Online.aspx

The American Council on Education (ACE) Military Guide presents ACE credit recommendations for formal courses and occupations offered by all branches of the military. All recommendations are based on ACE reviews conducted by college and university faculty members who are actively teaching in the areas they review. You can search for courses and occupations using the ACE identification number, military course number or title, training location, dates completed, or subject and level. New courses and occupations are continually being evaluated by ACE, and these entries are added on a daily basis. The Military Guide includes all evaluated courses and occupations from 1954 to the present.

### CAEL 10 Standards for Assessing Learning

http://www.cael.org/pla.htm#Follow the Ten Standards for Assessing Learning

Created in 1974 by the Council for Adult & Experiential Learning (CAEL), the Standards for Assessing Learning is the benchmark used by colleges and universities to assess prior learning.

### CLEP (College-Level Examination Program)

clep.collegeboard.org

Developed by the College Board, CLEP is the most widely accepted credit-by-examination program, its credits accepted at more than 2,900 colleges and universities. CLEP offers 33 standardized exams in a wide variety of academic subjects, including history, literature, science, mathematics, and business. The College Board is the same organization that develops the AP and SAT exams.

### DSST

getcollegecredit.com

DANTES Subject Standardized Test (DSST) offers 38 standardized exams in subjects such as Social Sciences, Math, Applied Technology, Business, Physical Sciences, and Humanities. DSST credits are recognized by more than 2,000 colleges and universities in the United States. DSST was formerly known as the DANTES (Defense Activity for Non-Traditional Education Support) Subject Standardized Tests.

### KNEXT.com

www.knext.com

KNEXT is an education software and solutions company whose Learning Recognition Program helps students identify their goals, document their learning, build a portfolio, and earn credit for the portfolio. KNEXT also helps higher education institutions build or enhance their prior learning assessment offerings and online portfolio management.

### Learning Counts

www.learningcounts.org

Launched by CAEL, Learning Counts helps adult learners earn college credit for non-traditional learning through the development and assessment of a portfolio.

## REFERENCES

American Council on Education. (2013). *Military guide.* Retrieved March 7, 2013 from http://www.acenet.edu/news-room/Pages/Military-Guide-Online.aspx

College Board. (2013). *About AP.* Retrieved March 7, 2013 from http://www.collegeboard.com/student/testing/ap/about.html

Council on Adult and Experiential Learning. (2013). *CAEL Standards of Quality Assurance in the Assessment of Prior Learning.* Retrieved May 31, 2013 from http://www.cael.org/pla.htm#Follow the Ten Standards for Assessing Learning.

Smith, P. (1986). *Your Hidden Credentials: the Value of Learning Outside of College.* Acropolis Books, Inc.

# CHAPTER 4

## Mapping Non-Traditional Learning through Portfolio Development

The United States has an adult population that has more experience that it has credentials: well-qualified, yet with knowledge and skills that are poorly recognized and underutilized in an economic and social environment that desperately needs its enhanced contributions. The question remains: What can we do to help adults update, recognize, and benefit from their experiential learning, helping not only themselves, but the country as a whole?

### DEVELOPING A PORTFOLIO FOR ASSESSMENT

As mentioned in Chapter 3, assessment via national or standardized exams is the most traditional method used to assess prior learning. Examinations are a great fit when the learning is straightforward and matches the subject discipline of the exam. However, this is not always the case. Fortunately, assessing prior learning by portfolio is becoming increasingly recognized and respected by higher education institutions.

A portfolio is a collection of evidence that supports a learner's claim for credit through a prior learning assessment process. It is a formal communication presented by the learner as part of a petition requesting credit or recognition for learning outside of the classroom setting. Colleges and universities may use different templates for portfolio development; some also use a formal prior learning course to guide students through the development of a portfolio. This chapter will guide through a formal process to document your learning, resulting in an actual document of your personal reflection.

There are multiple benefits to using a portfolio to assess your prior learning. As a practical matter, assessed learning that is counted towards the degree will save you time and money. At Kaplan University, for example, the average assessed portfolio was awarded almost one year's worth of credit toward the degree. This resulted not only in a time savings of almost one year, but also financial savings of almost $10,000 per person on average (Kaplan University 2013). Numbers are based on the total number of students who have passed EL 203 and submitted a portfolio for evaluation. Past performance is no guarantee of future results. Tuition savings calculated as 26 quarter credit hours x $371.00 = $9,646.00. Figures are provided for illustrative purposes and are not a guarantee that students will earn any particular number of credits or achieve any particular savings. Statements regarding credits received, reduced time to graduation, and tuition savings are as of January 2013.

In this chapter, you will learn how to analyze and document your experiences in an effort to extract the learning you have gained through them.

## GETTING STARTED: IDENTIFYING YOUR EXPERIENTIAL LEARNING

As we have emphasized so far, learning can be acquired through the experience of living. You have acquired learning through many years of work, as an employee, manager, or owner/operator of an organization, and life experiences such as caring for children or the elderly, and running a household. The key to earning recognition, and ultimately college credit, for your learning lies in your ability to recall, align, and document your learning to college-level courses. A map of your non-traditional learning to higher education can be articulated and documented in an experiential learning portfolio. These exercises will provide you with a review of various types of learning and in-depth information about portfolio development.

### College-level Learning vs. Experiential Learning

As you begin the process of reflection or recalling and documenting your prior learning, you need to understand the type of learning that you've acquired. You may have acquired learning at a college or university, from professional training, on-the-job training, or perhaps from training that led to a certification.

**College-level Learning** Learning is considered to be college-level if it meets the course outcomes or objectives for courses offered by regionally- or nationally-accredited colleges and universities. College-level learning is typically earned by taking courses directly from a college or university, meeting course objectives and outcomes.

**Experiential Learning** According to David Kolb (1984), experiential learning is any learning that results from a person's reflection on his or her experiences. This type of learning involves direct participation or observation. This is in contrast formal learning that occurs in a school-type setting. On-the-job training, a certification, and volunteer activities are all examples of experiential learning. Although, the hands-on learning provides a concrete or tangible learning, there is still learning that happens in tandem; we collect additional ideas and information in an intangible manner. We take the idea and learned information and test them to arrive at conclusions. Some learn by observation and some learn by doing. For example, you need to learn how to operate a new computer that you just purchased. Some people will read the manual, review the online video, and by asking others. Yet someone else might just turn on the computer and dive right into learning how it operates.

## REFLECTION: HOW YOU HAVE LEARNED OVER THE YEARS

Recall Kolb's definition of experiential learning as learning that results from a person's reflection on his or her experiences. Not just experience, but *reflection* on experience is key to this type of learning. When Allen Tough set out to do the research that led to his ground-breaking book *The Adult's Learning Projects*, he formulated a series of questions designed to help learners reflect: to think about the people, the institutions, the things, the events, and other devices that they have used to learn over the years. And as you reflect, you will also undoubtedly remember additional learning, recalling knowledge and skills that you may have forgotten or overlooked.

This exercise of reflection is like raking your lawn, collecting all the leaves (evidence of what resources you used to learn) while leaving the grass (non-learning events) behind. In the recall effort of reflection, think of the following major areas of your life: your home or your family; your hobbies or recreation; your job; your community responsibilities; and writing, research, teaching, or coaching. The key here is to go event by event, or year by year, then month by month, and actively remember *how you learned* and *what you did to learn.*

For example, think back over the past few years at how you may have learned using the following.

### Written Material

Can you recall times that you set out to learn something in particular by reading

- a book;
- newspapers or magazines;
- booklets, pamphlets, or brochures;
- memos, letters, instructions, or plans;
- technical or professional literature;
- material in a library; or
- workbooks or online instruction?

## Experts

Can you recall times that you set out to learn something in particular by consulting an expert such as a

- medical doctor;
- counselor or therapist;
- lawyer;
- financial or tax advisor;
- coach, or
- private teacher?

## Multimedia

Can you recall times that you set out to learn something in particular by

- watching or listening to the news;
- watching documentary films;
- listening to a radio program or podcast;
- searching for information on the Internet; or
- taking a self-directed course or "attending" lectures on DVD, CD, or the Internet?

## Conversations

Have you tried to learn from conversations or discussions with any of the following

- friends or family members;
- employees, colleagues, or supervisors; or
- other stimulating individuals?

## Groups

Have you learned through a group activity, such as

- a conference, retreat, or weekend meeting;
- an institute, short course, or workshop;
- a club or association meeting;
- work on a board or committee?

# THE MAPPING PROCESS: PORTFOLIO DEVELOPMENT

Now that you have a basic understanding of prior learning assessment, experiential learning, and college-level learning, you are ready to learn about the portfolio development process that you can use to create your experiential learning portfolio. You will need to understand this process in order to develop a portfolio that meets the requirements for submission, enabling you to earn credit for your learning.

The portfolio development process is both a reflective and a mechanical process. You will reflect on your life experiences and then organize and document the learning in an organized manner so that it can be evaluated by qualified subject matter experts.

In the portfolio development process, you will follow these steps:

1. Identify your educational goals to create an educational goal statement or essay.
2. Explore your prior learning and highlight your learning experiences to create an expanded resume format in chronological order.
3. Write about and document your learning to create a learning autobiography.
4. Search for college-level courses that match your learning to develop a course petition.
5. Gather documents to support your learning.

Each step is described below in more detail.

## Educational Goal Statement

The first step to attaining a goal is to actually establish one. An educational goal statement is simply a statement or short essay on what you plan to do with your education. Creating an educational goal statement is the beginning of the reflection that you will later demonstrate in your portfolio. In setting an educational goal, first think of what you plan to do in the next ten years: this will be your long-term goal. Then break your long-term goal into small, easy-to-accomplish chunks: these will be your short-term goals.

For the purpose of beginning your portfolio, focus your goal on your education. What information and skills do you need to help you achieve other goals, such as those related to your career? Do you have a short-term goal of updating your skills and a long-term goal of earning a degree? Include things like your reasons to return to school, what you hope to learn, and why.

To recap, an educational goal includes

- short-term goals,
- long-term goals,
- the reason for completing a degree or certificate, and
- how you plan to use the knowledge.

An example of an Educational Goal Statement is provided at the end of this chapter.

## Expanded Resume

Now that you've had an opportunity to reflect on how you have learned over the years, it's time to record and document the experiences in a formal manner. This exercise will help you expand your professional resume; it is called an expanded resume because it will contain much more information and detail than a typical resume for a job application. The information in the expanded resume can be divided into employment history, education and technical skills, professional activities, and extracurricular activities. As with a typical resume, you will

- Identify work and life experience from which you have acquired knowledge, skills, and abilities in chronological order.
- Organize your experiences according to the categories (employment history, education and technical skills, professional activities, and extracurricular activities).

## Learning Autobiography

A learning autobiography is chronological narrative or essay that describes what you have learned and how your learning has grown as a result. As previously mentioned, reflecting and remembering is a big part of the portfolio development process. Most people forget important moments and learning projects that they have undertaken. So, another approach to identifying your experiential learning is to write an account of your important experiences. In the beginning, don't worry about describing learning or skills. Simply describe important life experiences as they come back to you.

Begin your autobiography by adding to the learning statement that you created. From there, you will continue the essay in a chronological manner. Use your expanded resume as a guide as you develop a chronological account of your learning experiences.

Significant life experiences often build on one another. As you remember and list experiences, describe how one activity may have prepared you for others. Be sure to include experiences that have been significant to your personal development and learning. What you are striving for is to identify themes – short- and long-term experiences that carry common characteristics.

A strong Learning Autobiography has the following characteristics

- is clearly written, in chronological order,
- highlights your learning experiences,
- describes in detail your learning acquired from those experiences,
- describes in detail how your learning has grown as a result of those experiences, and
- clearly articulates how you have learned from your experiences.

An example of a learning autobiography is provided at the end of this chapter.

## Course Petitions

Now you're ready for the mechanical process of assembling and connecting your experiential learning with college-level courses. The learning autobiography is your reflective story; the next step is to develop course petitions to show how your acquired learning meets college standards.

A course petition is the component of the portfolio in which you will demonstrate that your learning is equivalent to college-level learning. It is your opportunity to show just how much you have learned through years of work and activities, and to make that learning count toward the completion of your college degree.

To develop your course petitions

- *Identify college-level courses that match your learning.* You can do this by visiting a college's website, browsing through a course catalog, or searching a college-level course database. First, search by course title, then review the course outcomes. Course outcomes or learning outcomes are statements that describe the knowledge, skills, and abilities that the learner can expect to attain by completing the course. Course outcomes are typically listed in a course syllabus or in the course catalog.
- *Connect sources of learning to a course petition.* A source of learning is where you actually experienced the learning. The source of learning is one of the experiences you listed in your expanded resume; it could be a position that you previously held, from a community activity, or from job training.
- *Create learning statements.* Learning statements are concise, brief statements that describe your prior learning as it relates to the courses that you are petitioning for. These learning statements will help you describe your learning in terms of how you met the course outcomes for each of the courses for which you are petitioning for credit. Examples of learning statements can be found at the end of this chapter.

  In your statements, be sure to use verbs that describe the cognitive level of your learning. (Refer to Bloom's Taxonomy, a classification system of learning goals, objectives, and achievements.)
- *Write a course petition.* A course petition is where you make the case that you have met the learning of an actual college-level course. After identifying a course that you think reflects the learning that you've acquired, you will build the petition to document that you've met the course objectives. The course petition should include course outcomes, sources of learning, and learning statements. Examples of Course Petitions are provided at the end of this chapter.

## Supporting Documentation

Supporting documentation ties the learning that you have described with actual work or evidence. The documentation is important because it provides evidence that the knowledge, skills, and abilities you have acquired are in fact college-level and aligned to the courses you are petitioning for. Supporting documentation includes

- Primary documentation: letters of verification written by people that have *first-hand* knowledge of your learning and are able to provide verification;
- Secondary documentation: any other information that can support your learning, including licenses, certificates, and project examples. Secondary documentation supplements your primary documentation with items such as original work samples that you've created including presentations, or reports.

## Top Tip: Gathering Your Supporting Documentation

The following helpful hints will assist you when gathering your supporting documentation:

- Start early!
- Select appropriate documentation such as licenses, certifications, and work samples. The documentation should connect specific learning with a college-level course.
- Avoid proprietary information. Proprietary information is any form of confidential information that is not readily available to the public. It could include things like a company's salary structure, a customer list, or content that you developed for a specific client (for example, privately developed software).
- Identify your references or sources. Your reference may be an expert in the field, a client that can attest to your abilities, or a supervisor.

## Key Terms

**Course Petition.** A document that shows how experiential learning maps to specific college-level courses

**Portfolio.** A collection of evidence that supports a learner's claim for credit

**Learning Autobiography.** A chronological, first-person narrative that describes what an individual has learned from experience and how their learning has grown

**Expanded Resume.** A detailed list of work and life experience from which a learner has acquired knowledge, skills, and abilities

# RESOURCES

### Bloom's Taxonomy

http://www.edpsycinteractive.org/topics/cognition/bloom.html

Bloom's taxonomy is a classification system of thinking and learning that can be used to develop learning statements.

# REFERENCES


Kolb, D. A. (1984). *Experiential learning: Experience as the source of learning and development.* Englewood Cliffs, NJ: Prentice Hall.

Smith, P. (1986). *Your Hidden Credentials: the Value of Learning Outside of College.* Acropolis Books, Inc. (117-120).

Tough, A. (1971). *The adult's learning projects: A fresh approach to theory and practice in adult learning.* Toronto: OISE.

# EDUCATIONAL GOAL STATEMENT SAMPLE

My educational goal is to eventually complete my Master's in International Finance. It has always been my ambition to be involved in stocks, bonds, and global trading. I'm currently enrolled in the Associate of Arts program with an emphasis on finance. The AA program leads directly into the Bachelors in Financial Management.

My interest first peeked when I started working part-time with my father in high school. He initially gave me the books to balance for his clients then I eventually was given the task of reviewing his stock and bond trades. I was immediately hooked and started learning about finance on my own. During the summer breaks, I took some independent stock classes at the local community college – which just reassured me that I had a future in finance.

I have had several part-time jobs with my father's financial advising company. I continued my bookkeeping work but also observed him with clients. I realize that to be respected and to get the job that I'd eventually like, I need the credentials required for the field. I'm currently studying to sit for my CFP (Certified Financial Planner). I will sit for it next year. That will give me a credential in addition to my degree.

I look forward to accomplishing all that I can in my degree process; this class, hopefully will help me gain valuable credit for learning that I've acquired. I am excited to be on my way to accomplishing my goals – I feel like they are within reach!

# SAMPLE EXPANDED RESUME

### Artistic Pursuits

Art Appreciation — June 1984 to Current

Developed an appreciation for all forms of visual art, working with interior designers on properties and as a Director of the Symphony Orchestra Design Showcase and the Melbourne Harbor Festival of Arts. Continue to attend and support diversified art exhibits.

Photography — August 1974 to Current

Photography and film development instruction as the high school yearbook photographer. Primarily engaged in digital and computer photographic programs now for business and personal pursuits.

Impressionist Art — June 1960 to Current

I have an impressive collection of all paintings and drawings by impressionist artist such as Monet, Cassatt and Sisley. I attend art meetings around the world to study the works of the impressionist.

### Computer/Technical Expertise

| | |
|---|---|
| Computer Systems Technician Diploma | January 2010 to March 2011 |
| Field Technician - Advanced | January 2006 to May 2006 |
| Technical Support Specialist | January 2003 to August 2004 |
| Network System Technician | March 2011 to Current |

### Employment History

XYZ Company
Fayetteville, GA United States
Truck Driver — May 2007 to Current

As owner-drive, I maintain shipping orders, receivables, payables, and deliveries; drive regular routes in the Southeast delivering orders on contract; manage customer database, write marketing and public relations information.

ABC Consulting
Jacksonville, FL United States
Self-Employed – Vice President — March 2012 to Current

Oversee client relations for higher education and corporate universities; manage company contracts, hire maintain faculty pool, write and provide work proposals, manage agreements; manage website presence; manage company receivables.

EBSCO Host
Seattle, WA United States
Director of Sales — March 1999 to May 2007

Manage customer requests; initiate customer calls; write up sales orders; follow up with customers to make sure deliverables were satisfactory; manage customer communication plan; oversee media development for customer interface.

### History, Cultural, or Regional Studies

History of Art — June 1999 to Current

Provided tours of local museums when impressionist art was on display.

MOSH April 2006 to 2009
Volunteer museum curator.

Art Research for local paper May 1999 to Current
Provided art research for continued articles to local newspaper.

Art Tours January 1999 to Current
Subject matter expert on tour with national museum to countries around the world.

International Travel January 1999 to Current
Family members live abroad, so I spend months in various countries learning about their art culture, history, and education.

### Religious and Spiritual Activities

First Presbyterian May 2000 to Current
Attend religious-art classes once per month. In addition, I sometimes fill in as class leader.

### Sports and Recreational Pursuits

Swimming (Intermediate) May 1995 to Current
Provide private swimming instructions to ages 3+; participate in regular team competition events for the city.

Yoga (Advanced) May 2004 to Current
Provide private instruction.

Shooting (Intermediate) January 1995 to Current
Recreational shooting; marksman competition; private instruction

### Volunteer Activities

American Association of Community Colleges (AACC) June 1999 to June 2007
Served as a member of the AACC Board; maintained membership records; solicited new members; made new member presentations.

### Languages

French
Speaking Level: Intermediate
Reading Level: Beginner
Writing Level: Beginner
Completed French I and French II with the ability to speak, read and write. After spending many months in France, I have secured this knowledge by self-study.

### Speaking Events

Museum Curator January 19, 2011
Event/Conference: Monthly art lectures
Role: Presenter
Organization: Jacksonville Museum.
Description: As museum curator, I provided monthly presentations on the art exhibits, primarily from the impressionist era.

Art History Lectures June 13, 2012
Event/Conference: City of Jacksonville Art Walk
Role: Featured Speaker
Organization: Chamber of Commerce
Description: As the local museum curator, I provided monthly talks on impressionist art at the Art Walk Events.

### Associations

Society of Human Resource Management July 1995 to Current
Professional

Chamber of Commerce January 2008 to Current
Professional

National Association of Museums August 1979 to Current
Professional

### Accomplishments

Association of Realtors May 2005 to July 2008
As Chair of the EP County Association of Realtors RPAC Committee received an annual recognition award for meeting and exceeding all RPAC fundraising goals in terms of amount of funds raised and percentage of membership participating.

Certified Real Estate Brokerage Management Magazine May 2008 to July 2008
Selected as a feature writer for the "Coaching Corner"

EP County Association of Realtors May 2008 to July 2008
Recipient of the Young Outstanding Political Achievement Award

Corral Ranch May 1990 to July 1990
Received Today's "Best" Award for being voted the best Western Wear store in Albany County by its readers

# LEARNING AUTOBIOGRAPHY SAMPLE

In the mid 90's, I began working with my father at his business. He was a Financial Planner; he manages financial portfolios for over 120 clients. At first, he let me simply do accounting-type work by reviewing numbers, checking the balances for accuracy, and creating ledger sheets. I loved the work as I have always been interested in numbers and how they numbers completed a bigger picture, like with balance and ledger sheets. The work for my father's business continued through high school. I eventually got to observe him in meetings with clients and insight into their financial portfolios.

During my summers in high school, I completed many independent finance-related training courses at the community college. Many of them were simply lower-level accounting, understanding ledgers, and basic stock trading information. This only solidified my decision to enter the community college's program for Financial Planners which led to an Associate of Arts with a financial emphasis. After my second semester, I applied for an advanced start program at the University to pursue my Bachelors in Financial Management. I completed my community college courses early and was able to transfer right into my Bachelors program.

During that time, I managed to secure a part-time position with a financial trading firm. This gave me insight into the world of stocks, bonds, and trading. While I loved working directly with people, as a financial planner, I really grew to love the experience and opportunity that the stock and bond markets offered. After two years of part-time work, I was finally offered a full-time position as a junior trader. This wasn't exactly the position I was interested in, but it gave me more insight into what actually goes on during a trading day. Although at times, it was energetic and exciting, there were many nights of long, hard work researching the financial position of companies, researching the performance of particular stocks and bonds, and then assembling all the research. I impressed my boss with my ability to conduct and provide accurate research; he eventually promoted me to Senior Accountant.

As Senior Accountant, I gained the experience of managing people. I gained insight into being an effective manager however; I realized that I needed more mentoring and training. My boss introduced me to one of his most effective managers; I was able to shadow him for a few months to gain more insight into managing people.

In August, 1999, after a year as a Senior Accountant, I was offered another promotion, but this time; it included a move to New York. The firm needed someone with my stock and bond insight to fill a critical open position on the trading floor. I accepted the position and was off to New York.

At the firm in New York, I was Senior Advisor, managing over 300 accounts. I had about 45 portfolio managers that reported to me. This position really stretched my skills and abilities, but I learned additional insights into the world of stock trading. I conducted domestic and foreign stock sales, became knowledgeable about compliance as well as international regulatory standards.

During that first year, I my manager recommended me for a side-job as editor for a stock trading magazine. I provided a weekly article to a stock magazine. The articles featured a weekly stock pick and provided research about that particular stock.

In 2003, after a few years of experience, I was ready to pursue my CFP (Certified Financial Planner). I began studying at the local community college. After completing the program, I started studying for my CFP examination. I joined and worked with a local study group for about 6 months before I felt that I was ready to sit for the exam. I passed on the first try!

In January 2004, my manager advised me of a position that would be open in the future. However, that position requires a Master's degree. So, I accelerated my degree process and completed my Bachelors so that I could enroll in the Master's program. I only needed a few courses to finish my Bachelors and continued right into my Master's program. I didn't want to miss this opportunity; so I continued my studies at an accelerated pace in addition to working 40 hours!

Late in 2005, as I was well into my Master's program, I decided to leave the firm, move back home, and start my own business. As much as I enjoyed my experience and all of the things that I learned as a stock broker in New York, I realized that I longed for a different lifestyle. Upon my return home, I joined the local Small Business Association (SBA) to learn all the specifics of starting my own business. I also used this as a networking opportunity to learn from other small business owners who had already gotten past the start-up phase. I took several classes at the SBA to gain insight into the local government, state laws, and financial options of a new start-up.

In 2007, I assumed a position with the local Chamber of Commerce as the small-business manager. This offered me the opportunity to help other small business owners when they relocated to the city. I was able to pass on to others the results of my many years of being mentored, learning from larger businesses, then being able to share my personal experience of starting my own business.

Today, I am a happy business owner, doing what I love by helping people manage their money. I've developed many financial plans, arranged college accounts, and have hired a wonderful team of financial managers. I keep my toes in the stock market with a few clients, helping them develop a strategy to buy and sell.

# SAMPLE LEARNING STATEMENTS

Below are examples of learning statements that describe a student's learning as it relates to a college course.

**Note:** These learning statements do not include the full list of learning statements to meet the course outcomes of these courses. The samples below are just examples.

Course: ACT 2021 – Financial Accounting

- Prepare financial statements
- Interpreting financial information for decision-making
- Control routine operations (budgeting and standard costing)

Course: ARH 1000 – Art Appreciation

- Use various forms of media to develop client brochures
- Identify key forms and elements of art to create 2D and 3D media
- Define materials and techniques needed for specialty projects

Course: DIG 2113 – Fundamentals of Digital Media

- Developed web animation using digital tools
- Create interfaces for site navigation
- Create 3D animation on client sites

Course: OST 1336 – Fundamentals of Business Communications

- Organized the company's business communications
- Develop, format, proofread and edit company's client communications
- Manage company's client communication plan, including presentations and business correspondence

# COURSE PETITION SAMPLES

| COURSE PETITION - MT 201: INTRODUCTION TO MANAGEMENT | | |
|---|---|---|
| **Course Outcomes** | **Source of Learning** | **Learning Statements** |
| By the end of this course, you should be able to:<br>* Describe solutions to management problems<br>* Recognize the four functions of management<br>* Explain the steps to manage change<br>* Understand competitiveness and collaboration in a global economy<br>* Demonstrate college-level communication through the composition of original materials in Standard American English<br>* Distinguish among different theoretical perspectives in the social sciences | IMG Consulting<br>January 2006 – October 2008 | * Understand four primary functions of management<br>* Utilize problem-solving techniques<br>* Schedule quarterly staff meetings to identify and resolve potential issues<br>* Maintain professionalism and effectiveness in the workplace<br>* Managed ethical and legal issues as they arose<br>* Developed new business concepts for the launch of new products<br>* Evaluated and facilitated the SWOT Analysis for projects |
| | United Support Systems,<br>October 2008 – Present | * Understand and manage with a global competiveness objectivity<br>* Manage daily audits of employee feedback; ensuring that employees received the appropriate feedback and instruction<br>* Oversee conflict resolution on projects<br>* Prepared project schedules, ensuring that timelines stayed on track<br>* Delegated and managed work responsibilities<br>* Developed clear channels of communication |

| COURSE PETITION - IT 190: FOUNDATIONS IN INFORMATION TECHNOLOGY | | |
|---|---|---|
| **Course Outcomes** | **Source of Learning** | **Learning Statements** |
| By the end of this course, you should be able to:<br>* Demonstrate operating systems software functionality<br>* Perform personal computer maintenance<br>* Describe the basic components of a computer network<br>* Understand competiveness and collaboration in a global economy<br>* Practice verbal communication by presenting ideas to others<br>* Identify ethical issues within the field of study | IMG Consulting<br>January 2006 –<br>October 2008 | * Solved computer software and hardware issues by problem solving and testing<br>* Installed operating systems<br>* Provided training on operating systems software<br>* Provided personal computer (PC) maintenance<br>* Provided troubleshooting efforts for computers, printers, desktop, and laptop devices |

| | | |
|---|---|---|
| | United Support Systems,<br>October 2008 – Present | * Presented technology updates at quarterly meetings<br>* Presented ethical or compromising case studies at the quarterly meetings<br>* Maintained the computer network system for over 1,000 PCs<br>* Planned and installed software and hardware upgrades |

| COURSE PETITION – AC 122: PAYROLL ACCOUNTING | | |
|---|---|---|
| **Course Outcomes** | **Source of Learning** | **Learning Statements** |
| By the end of this course, you should be able to:<br>* Explain the characteristics of a good record keeping system<br>* Describe the major applications of the Fair Labor Standards Act<br>* Calculate social security taxes on individual incomes<br>* Calculate withholding allowances for income tax purposes<br>* Evaluate the factors that determine unemployment eligibility<br>* Prepare payroll registers and employee earnings records | Any Corporation<br>May 2005 – April 2011 | * Manage payroll process for over 500 salaried and contract employees<br>* Use and oversee the ADP Payroll Services<br>* Maintain the payroll system to accurately reflect employee working and leave hours<br>* Processed and ensured quality and accuracy of the payroll data<br>* Ensured accurate payroll deductions<br>* Managed the 401k and other employee savings programs<br>* Trained staff on the Fair Labor Standards Act; provided quarterly updated<br>* Managed unemployment process ensuring eligibility; responded to unemployment claims<br>* Reconciled payroll reports monthly<br>* Oversee conflict resolution regarding payroll issues |

# CHAPTER 5

## Selecting a Certificate or Degree Program That Fits

Most adults go back to school in order to earn a certificate or degree in a particular field. Selecting a certificate or degree program can be a daunting task for anyone, especially an adult learner. With so many choices, and terminology like *transfer credit, core requirements, degree audit,* and *electives*, knowing where to start and how to select a degree program can be overwhelming and confusing.

The truth is that most adult learners are not equipped with the information and resources that can help them make an informed decision when selecting a degree program. Furthermore, many are not even aware of what they don't know. So, how do we discover what we don't know?

This chapter will cover the major questions that should be answered in order to determine what you need in a degree program, along with a glossary of terms associated with degree programs. Our busy lives and schedules often lead us toward making decisions by taking the easy road, which when choosing degree program that fits could be a mistake. Inquiry thorough research and careful deliberation are crucial to selecting a program that will pay off for you in the end.

# OVERVIEW OF PROGRAM OPTIONS

Today, you have many choices when selecting a degree program. Not only are there many options when it comes to the degree focus, there are also choices regarding the type of degree, the format of the program, and the purpose of the degree.

People tend to select a college first and then select a program available at the college. There is nothing wrong with this process; however, if you want a specific degree focus, selecting the college first may lead you in the wrong direction. We feel strongly that it is important to consider the degree program options and figure out what you need in the program before selecting a college or university.

The following describes the major program areas within colleges and universities.

## Vocational or Technical Education

Vocational or technical education helps prepare students for a specific job or trade such as cosmetology, funeral services, fashion, automotive, or information technology. Vocational training is often associated with hands-on learning through internships. While vocation or technical studies do not result in a college-level degree, many result in a level of certification. It is important to know that vocational and technical coursework is not transferrable to undergraduate or graduate degrees should you decide to continue your education.

## Undergraduate Education

Undergraduate education includes postsecondary education at the associate and bachelor's levels. The associate degree includes the first two years of an undergraduate degree. According to a 2012 report by the U.S. Bureau of Labor Statistics, someone with an associate degree has greater earning potential than those with only a high school diploma. A bachelor's degree, typically earned as a result of a four-year study, has a wide variety of subjects and length. Both associate and bachelor's degrees are college-credit bearing degrees and are typically transferrable to other colleges or universities in the event you continue your education at the graduate level.

## Graduate Education

Graduate education includes degrees at the master's and doctoral levels. Students must have successfully earned a bachelor's degree to be eligible to enter a graduate program. Graduate degrees are required by some professions, such as those in education and health-related fields.

## Professional Education

Professional education usually requires the completion of an undergraduate or graduate degree before starting and will lead to a certification or a license such as law, medicine, or veterinary medicine.

# CHOOSING A DEGREE PROGRAM

Once you've selected a college and submitted an application, you will be assigned an academic advisor who will guide you through the degree selection process. However, there are a few questions that you should consider before meeting with your advisor. (The following questions can also be found in a worksheet at the end of this chapter.)

## Goals

*What are your short- and long-term educational, professional, and personal goals? What is the purpose of your degree? How does it fit in with your goals?*

First and foremost, you should determine the purpose for earning your degree. What do you expect as a result of earning the degree? Do you want to learn new skills? Do you need the degree to advance in your career? Or do you simply want it for self-fulfillment –to, for example, be a college graduate? Determining your purpose or the end-goal of your degree is the first step in selecting a degree that is the best fit for you. You should keep this question in mind as you are making your other decisions.

## Purpose

*What is the purpose of the degree or certification?*

This is associated with your short- and long-term goals. How will the degree or certification help you accomplish your goals? As with your goals, you must keep the purpose of your degree in mind to keep you on target; it's easy to get distracted with the prospect of a new, flashy degree that sounds good.

## Interests

*What field or subject-area are you interested in pursuing?*

Again, associated with your short- and long-term goals, is there something that you are interested in studying, such as information technology, criminal justice, or journalism? It's important to keep your personal interest in mind as you plan for the future. For some adult learners, it's not just about acquiring a degree but pursuing something that is of interest.

## Type of Degree

*What type of degree do you want or need? Does your career field require a degree? Does your career or the job you want require a certain level of degree?*

As you begin narrowing down your list, the type of degree matters. First, are you simply interested in acquiring skills to gain employment or do you want a professional degree or license? Second, what is required for your career? What degree does your dream job require or what is required for promotion? Keeping this question in mind during your decision making helps you stay on focus. A graduate degree sounds prestigious and important, but if it is not what you need, you could be wasting time and money.

## Accreditation

*Do you need a degree with a specialized certification, licensing, or accreditation? If you need the degree for career purposes, does it need to carry a particular accreditation?*

Some professional degrees require that graduates from specific programs are professionally qualified and competent, or professionally accredited. For example, some financial institutions require the Certified Financial Planner (CFP) designation. The Accreditation Council for Business Schools & Programs (ACBSP) is a recognized accreditation for business schools.

## Previous Credits

*Have you previously attended any college or university and have credit for transfer?*

The answer to this question is important because you need to know where your starting point is. By gathering all of your previous college transcripts, you can identify courses you've completed; this will give you an idea of what is remaining to complete the degree that you are interested in. You don't want to repeat courses that you may have successfully completed in the past. Not only is repeating a course frustrating, it will also cost you time and money.

### Top Tip: Official Transcripts

Official transcripts are usually sent from one institution to another institution to be evaluated. Once evaluated, the credits eligible for transfer are placed on your transcript. In the event of a delay in recording your official transcripts, you can keep moving forward with advising with the unofficial copies. Either print an unofficial copy or request an additional copy for yourself.

Once you receive your copy of your transcript, review them to determine what courses you've completed and how much transfer credit do you have. This will give you an idea of what you'll need to take to complete a degree, how much time it will take, and how much money you'll need to finance the degree.

## Prior Learning

*Do you have any on-the-job training, military training, certification, professional, or experiential learning that could be worth college-level credit?*

Identifying any potential learning or experience that may be at the college-level can save you time and money. For example, if you worked in a position where you received on-the-job training or certifications, you definitely want to utilize (and not repeat) that learning toward your degree program. You can refer to Chapters 3 and 4 for more detailed information on prior learning assessment (PLA), or earning credit for learning that occurs outside the traditional classroom. Gather any potential training that could be at the college-level; it can help save tuition while shortening your time to graduation.

## Learning Experience

*What mode of instruction is most preferable to you? What type of learning environment do you feel the most comfortable in? Are you a visual learner? Are you an independent learner?*

Given the fact that you will have to spend time outside the classroom studying, conducting research, and completing assignments (in addition to work and personal life), you need to consider if you have the time and flexible schedule required to dedicate to a face-to-face classroom. If not, maybe an online or hybrid option is right for you. There are a number of different program options. You need to select the type of class that best suits you and your schedule.

**Online Programs** Online programs are delivered via the Internet. Students access coursework, turn in assignments, and communicate with faculty and classmates using a mobile device such as a computer. An online program may be a good fit if you consider yourself an independent learner. Being an independent learner means taking the initiative to keep up, complete assignments without guidance, complete tasks on time, and seek out answers for yourself. An online program may also be a good fit if you feel comfortable with information and communications technology. However, even if you are wary of technology, you may want to consider it. Online learning has come a long way; today's classes are very interactive, provide lots of visual aids, and also include lots of student and instructor interaction. Online learning may also be a good fit if you are trying to go to school while you are working, managing family obligations, and trying to have a life.

**Traditional Programs** Traditional, face-to-face classes might be more to your liking if you really rely on the interaction with an instructor and enjoy the personal interaction with your classmates.

**Hybrid Programs** If you enjoy face-to-face interactions, but also value the flexibility of online programs, ask about hybrid programs. A hybrid program is a mixture of both the traditional and online. The program will have a mixture of classes that may be online, face-to-face, or both. Some programs meet at the beginning and end of a program with the rest being in an online format.

## Timeframe

*What is your timeframe? How much time do you have to set aside to meet your educational goals?*

Degrees, certifications, and programs come in different sizes; and in this case, one size does not fit all. Courses leading to a degree can be the traditional length of 15–16 weeks or you may prefer the accelerated version which last six–eight weeks. Just be aware of your options so that you can align them with your timeframe for earning the degree.

### Budget

*What is your budget?*
You will need to decide if you have the funds to contribute to your education or will rely on financial aid. You can refer to Chapter 8 for more in-depth detail on financing on your education.

## NEXT STEPS

Hopefully these questions have helped you realize the different things that could affect You may find that some questions don't apply to you at all, and that's fine.

Once you've answered these questions, you will need to assess which criteria are most important to you. It is possible that no single program will meet all of your needs to the extent that you hope they will. Rating the criteria based on their importance to you will help you make the best decision possible.

Determining what you need in a degree program is the first step toward selecting a college. There are a few things that you can take care of before you move on to the next step of selecting a college (Chapter 6).

1. Make a list of all colleges that you've previously attended. Once you've selected your potential colleges, you can begin requesting official transcripts.
2. Brush up on writing and technology skills. If you have not been to school in a while, you may need to brush up on college-level writing. In addition, technology in the classroom is very different from how it was just a few years ago. You may need to brush up on technology in the classroom.
3. Start your financial plan; determine your eligibility for financial assistance (See Chapter 8).
4. Begin the search for a college or university that has your selected degree program.

## SUMMARY

Own your leaning! Your degree choice will have a direct impact on your future, so do your research and ask yourself questions when determining which degree is the best fit. Do you need it for your career path? Do you want the quickest path to a degree? What degree level is necessary? You may already be established in a career path; is so, your decision will be relatively easier. However, if you plan to factor in a future career change to possibly coincide with personal interests, you have more things to consider.

Selecting your degree is only one step in completing your educational goal; the next step will be to select a college or university that provides the degree or certification that you are looking for. The next chapter, *Selecting a college or university that's right for you*, will get you started on that next step.

## Key Terms

**Accreditation.** The process by which an independent organization (an accrediting agency) assesses an educational institution or program to determine whether or not it meets educational standards

**Certification.** A certification represents a level of knowledge or skills attainment, as recognized officially by a certification-granting institution.

**Core course.** A fundamental course of a particular degree program

**Credit Transfer.** The procedure by which college credit taken at one institution is recognized and accepted by another institution

**Degree audit.** An analysis of a student's progress toward a degree

**Electives.** A group of courses within a degree program that are not specifically required for the degree (also known as general electives, open electives, or free electives)

**General education course.** Courses that are common to all degree programs and include subjects such as english composition, math, science, history, government, and arts (also referred to as "gened" courses)

**Hybrid course.** A course that includes a mixture face-to-face elements and other formats such as online or self-paced (also referred to as a blended course)

**Major.** The subject, or discipline, focus of a program or degree

**Minor.** A secondary subject, or discipline, focus of a program or degree

**Transfer Credit.** The actual credit earned at one college or university that is transferred to another college or university

## REFERENCES

Bureau of Labor Statistics. (2012). Earnings and employment rates by educational attainment. Retrieved from http://www.bls.gov/emp/ep_chart_001.htm

# DECIDING ON A DEGREE PROGRAM

## Worksheet

Use the following worksheet as a guide to help you through the questions to consider when selecting a degree program.

1. What are your short- and long-term educational, professional, and personal goals?

| Educational Goals | Professional Goals | Personal Goals |
|---|---|---|
| | | |

2. What is the purpose of the degree or certification?

3. What field or subject-area are you interested in pursuing?

4. What type of degree do you want or need?

- ❑ Vocational or Technical Education
- ❑ Undergraduate Education
- ❑ Graduate Education
- ❑ Professional Education

5. Do you need a degree with a specialized certification, licensing, or accreditation? If so, what are the requirements?

6. Have you previously attended any college or university and have credit for transfer?

   List your previously attended colleges, courses, and credits earned.

| College | Course | Credits Earned |
|---|---|---|
| | | |
| | | |
| | | |
| | | |
| | | |
| | | |
| | | |
| | | |
| | | |
| | | |

7. Do you have any on-the-job training, military training, certification, or professional or experiential learning that could be worth college-level credit?

| Training Source | Description |
|---|---|
| | |
| | |
| | |
| | |
| | |
| | |
| | |

8. What mode of instruction is most preferable to you?
   - ❑ I am more comfortable in a face-to-face environment that is instructor led. (Traditional classroom)
   - ❑ I prefer the online environment where I can study on my own schedule. (Online program)
   - ❑ I prefer a combination of both face-to-face and flexible meeting times. (Hybrid programs)

9. What is your time frame for completing the program?
   - ❑ Less than 1 year
   - ❑ 2 – 3 years
   - ❑ 4 + years

10. How do you plan to finance your education?
    - ❑ I don't have a budget.
    - ❑ A mixture of self-pay and financial aid.
    - ❑ I will rely on financial aid.
    - ❑ I will pay.

11. What is your budget?

# CHAPTER 6

## Selecting a College or University That Fits

Selecting a college or university is a big decision. Whether you are starting college for the first time or returning to finish a degree, deciding on the college that is the best fit for you can be a daunting task. With so many options, it can be hard to know where to begin. Selecting and deciding on a college or university should entail a similar process as you would use when making a major purchase. As a consumer making a major purchase, you would research, ask questions, and then do more research before making a final decision.

As with any consumer-based decision, a good place to begin is by looking toward the end: what do you want as an end result? What product do you want to walk away with? Do you want a certificate, a degree, new skills, or just new knowledge?

With more than 4,000 degree-granting colleges and universities in the United States (Higher Education: Institutions and Enrollment, 2012), it can be hard to know where to begin when selecting a college. It is not always immediately apparent how these institutions differ from each other. Two institutions that seem very similar may be different in crucial ways that can affect what you can get out of them.

This chapter covers some of the major features of higher education institutions that you should consider when choosing a school. These include the types of schools, types of accreditation, enrollment, graduation rates, and other school-specific information. Because there are more choices now than ever before, it is beneficial to be familiar with things that could potentially affect you. Even if you have a school in mind, it's useful to review the steps to support your decision.

## EIGHT STEPS TO CHOOSING THE RIGHT COLLEGE

The following eight steps will help guide you through the decision-making process to determine the right 'fit.' (These criteria are also available in worksheet form at the end of this chapter.)

### Step 1: Get Started!

Taking the first step is the hardest with any important decision. But after you take that first step, the following steps will be easier. Life is busy with work, family, friends, travel, etc., and is unlikely to change. Take time for yourself; take the first step toward attaining your educational goals. Get started by setting a goal of when you would like to start school.

### Step 2: Decide What Your Goals Are for Going to School

*Do you want to finish or start a degree? Are you looking for an industry-specific certification that will make you more marketable or employable? Do you want to take classes to prepare you for another degree program or to help you run your business? Determine your ultimate end-goal. If your long-term goal isn't really clear for you, then determine what your short-term goal is. Do you want to brush up on your computer skills or learn more about economics?* You need to know where you are going to make plans to move in the right direction. Using the Worksheet, write down the goals that you want to accomplish by returning to school. Refer to Chapter 6 for more information on selecting a degree program.

### Step 3: Understand the Options That Are Available to You

With so many variations of higher education institutions, you should be familiar with your various options to select the best fit for you. As you begin researching the institutions that you are interested in, you will find that there are many options available.

Type of School There are a number of different types of schools. Note that a particular school can fall into more than one category.

- *Public schools*, whether they are two-year or four-year, were founded by and are supported by state government and are managed by appointed boards or trustees. The institutions typically have lower tuition rates than non-public schools because they are supported by state funds. Because state funds are involved, public institutions have both in-state and an out-of-state tuition rates. The guidelines for in-state and out-of-state rates vary at institutions. If you have lived in a particular state for less than a year, you should ask about the qualifications for in-state tuition.

- *Private schools* receive little or no money subsidies from the government. Tuition tends to be higher at private schools but also tends to be the same regardless if you are in-state or out-of-state. Private schools are also typically owned by private individuals or group. Private colleges and universities may be non-profit or for-profit organizations.
- *For-profit schools,* also known as proprietary education, are institutions operated by private, profit-seeking organizations or companies.
- *Independent schools* are privately owned and managed, setting their own policies. They do not receive state funds, and thus tuition is generally higher than in public institutions. Independent and private schools tend to have more limited degree options than other schools; however they provide a smaller, more personal atmosphere.
- *Professional and technical schools* focus on workforce training, providing students with skills required for specific occupations. The schools offer full- and part-time programs for employment, training or retraining to improve skills, and apprenticeships training. The programs range from weeks to years, depending on the training. Program completion typically results in a license, a certification, or an associate of applied science (AAS) degree.
- *Career schools,* often known as technical, vocational, or trade schools, are even more career-focused than professional and technical schools. They are designed to specifically teach the skills needed for a job or a trade such as cosmetology, medical imaging, or plumbing through hands-on training and experience.

**Type of Instructional Delivery** *How do you learn the best? Do you feel more comfortable in an online, self-paced class or in a face-to-face with interaction with other students and instructors?* Selecting the type of delivery that best fits you can increase your chances of success whether it's a face-to-face class or an online environment. Some colleges and universities only offer traditional face-to-face instruction; some only offer online instruction; and some offer a mixture of face-to-face, online, and hybrid classes and programs. Refer to Chapter 6 for in-depth description of the various types of instructional delivery.

**Accreditation.** Accreditation is a process that is is not understood by most learners, but is one of the most important to the learner in that it affects the transferability or acceptance of the degree program by other colleges or by employers. The purpose of the accreditation process is to ensure that the education provided by the accreditor's member institutions meet an acceptable and consistent level of quality. Accreditation is a voluntary process that colleges and universities can elect to participate in. Accreditation guidelines and policies vary by accreditors, so it's important to be aware of accreditation agencies. The accreditation guidelines and policies can affect the transfer, acceptance, and recognition of your degree by other schools or industries.

While the US. Department of Education does not govern the accreditation process, it does publish a list of nationally recognized accrediting agencies that are determined to be credible and reliable. It is also important to know that accreditation is not permanent. Schools have to reapply periodically and can lose their accreditation.

## Top Tip: Accreditation

Below are a few brief topics to help you become familiar with accreditation agencies and how you could possibly be affected.

- **Program vs. Institutional Accreditation** There are basically two types of accreditation, program and institution. The program accreditation applies to specific programs within a college or university, such as a business or nursing degree. The institutional accreditation evaluates the institution as a whole and is provided by regional and national accreditation agencies.
- **Regional Accreditation** Regional accreditation agencies provide accreditation to schools located in a specific geographic region of the United States. Regionally accredited schools are primarily academically-focused institutions and tend to accept transcripts only from other regional institutions.
- **Middle States Association of Colleges and Schools** www.msche.org
  **New England Association of Colleges and Schools** www.neasc.org
  **North Central Association of Colleges and Schools** www.ncahigherlearningcommission.org
  **Northwest Commission on Colleges and Universities** www.nwccu.org
  **Southern Association of Colleges and Schools** www.sacs.org
  **Western Association of Schools and Colleges** www.wascweb.org
- **National Accreditation** National accreditation agencies cover specific types of schools or programs rather than geographical areas. For example,
  - **The Distance Education and Training Council (DETC)**
    (Accredits postsecondary institutions that offer online degree programs) www.detc.org
  - **The Accrediting commission of Career Schools and Colleges of Technology (ACCSCT)**
    (Accredits career schools and technology programs) www.accsc.org

**Specialized accreditation agencies**. Specialized accreditation agencies provide program-based accreditation that covers programs like allied health, business, pharmacy, or veterinary medicine. A complete list of specialized, program-based accreditors can be found in the Council for Higher Education Accreditation Resource.

**Accreditation and Financial Aid** In addition to transfer issues, the type of accreditation may influence your opportunities for grants or federal financial aid. In general, you will not be eligible for federal financial aid when attending an unaccredited institution. Chapter 8 provides a much more in-depth review of educational financing, including federal funding.

**Unaccredited Institutions** Since accreditation is on a volunteer basis, some schools choose not to be reviewed. Lack of accreditation is not necessarily an indication of poor quality in a program or institution. However, it can certainly present significant problems for students when it comes to credit transfer, degree recognition, and financial aid. Other schools or employers may not recognize degrees earned at unaccredited schools. You can check on the accreditation status of a single school's accreditation or you can search for schools that have a specific specialization at the U.S. Department of Education's Database of Accredited Postsecondary Institutions and Programs.

For more detailed information on accreditation, see the links provided in the Resources section.

**Policy on Prior Learning Assessment** Prior learning assessment (PLA) policies will differ with each school. You need to be aware that PLA is not just a single method of assessing or recognizing college-level learning, but instead encompasses multiple types of assessments. The more recognized methods include credit by exam such as CLEP and DSST; Challenge Exams; ACE Credit Recommendations; and prior learning assessment, sometimes referred to as Portfolio Development and Assessment. Schools may accept none, one, some, or all of these methods. See Chapter 4 for more information and detail on the various methods of prior learning assessment.

**Cost** Part of your decision in returning to school definitely involves the cost. As tuition can range from less than $100 per credit hour to over $300 per credit hour, the decision surrounding cost begins with selecting a college. Refer to Chapter 8 for more information on financing your education.

**General Institutional Characteristics** While your decision may not depend on any one of the institutional facts, the facts do collectively provide insight to the quality, results, and integrity of the schools. Web sites like the College Navigator provide a one-stop shop for institution information. The information required by the US Department of Education is part of required reporting by the schools. General information about a school includes

- **Academic focus.** Some schools have limited degrees or programs, providing an academic focus on specific areas. Also be aware that a school might offer a particular degree, but not consider it a specialty of the school.
- **Enrollment.** If class size is an important factor for you, check out the school's enrollment. If you cannot find a school's enrollment or faculty-to-student ratio on the schools website, that information is available on the College Navigator.
- **Graduation rates.** A school's graduation rate probably reveals more about the school than any other characteristic. While graduation rate may not be indicative of the quality of the degree, it could reflect the availability of services and support that promote student success.
- **Job placement rates.** If the purpose of earning your degree is job-related, this factor could be important to you. In addition to requesting the job placement rate from your list of prospective schools, there are various web resources to find the information yourself, such as the *U.S. News & World Report* annual education reports. When reviewing the job placement rates, make sure that the placement is in the field of interest, not just any job.

## Step 4: Rate the Criteria in Order of Importance When Selecting a School

It's time to rank the list discussed in Step 3. Based on options that you selected, rank your preferences so you can focus only on the criteria that is most important to you.

## Step 5: Develop a List of Possible Schools and Request Information from Each

Now that you are armed with some general information about selecting a college or university that is a good fit, it's time to make your list of prospective schools that meet the important criteria you have identified. Once you have a list, request information from each of them. Schools typically have a standard information package that is either available online or can be mailed to you. The package will include information about degree programs, application, and enrollment.

## Step 6: Research, Investigate, and Research More

Be an informed consumer. Apply the previous steps to the prospective schools on your list, beginning with your goal in mind. If you can't readily locate the accreditation, transfer, or financial aid information on the school's website, make a phone call. The school should be more than willing to answer your questions. You might even consider a visit to the school during an open house, meet the staff, meet the faculty, and possibly even talk to alumni.

## Step 7: Apply to Your Top Choices

Once you have an opportunity to sift through your research on each school, it's time to submit your application to several schools. Because some programs and schools have limited application windows, begin this process as early as possible. Be aware that the admission process can vary from school to school. Find out as early as possible what information is required for your application. You will need to have time to collect transcripts, recommendations, and test scores.

## Step 8: Select Your School!

Enjoy your educational experience and look forward to the reward at the end.

### Key Terms

**Accreditation.** The process by which an independent organization (an accrediting agency) assesses an educational institution or program to determine whether or not it meets educational standards

**Prior Learning Assessment (PLA).** Methods of earning college credit for experiential learning (learning acquired outside a traditional classroom; methods include exam and portfolio development

## WEB RESOURCES

U.S. News and World Report, Best College Rankings and Lists
http://colleges.usnews.rankingsandreviews.com/best-colleges/rankings
You can browse college rankings provided annually by the *U.S. News and World Report*.

### College Navigator

http://nces.ed.gov/collegenavigator/

Supported by the National Center for Education Statistics (NCES), the College Navigator is a search tool you can use to locate information and demographics on higher education institutions.

### Database of Accredited Postsecondary Institutions and Programs

http://ope.ed.gov/accreditation/

You can search this US Department of Education database by a specific institution or you can download all accredited institutions.

### U.S. Department of Education: Accreditation in the United States

http://www2.ed.gov/admins/finaid/accred/index.html

ED.gov is a US Department of Education site for information on accreditation in the United States.

### U.S. Department of Education: Regional and National Institutional Accrediting Agencies

http://www2.ed.gov/admins/finaid/accred/accreditation_pg6.html

This website provides more information about the regional or national accrediting agencies recognized by the Secretary of Education.

### Council for Higher Education Accreditation

http://www.chea.org/Directories/regional.asp

A national advocate and institutional voice for self-regulation of academic quality through accreditation, CHEA is an association of 3,000 degree-granting colleges and universities and recognizes 60 institutional and programmatic accrediting organizations.

### U.S. Department of Education: About Federal Student Aid

https://www2.ed.gov/admins/finaid/about/edpicks.jhtml?src=ln

This collection of resources will provide you with more in-depth information on student aid.

### Distance Education and Training Council (DETC)

www.detc.org

DETC is a non-profit education association that accredits distance learning institutions.

## REFERENCES

United States Census Bureau. (2012). Higher Education: Institutions and Enrollment, 2012. Retrieved from http://www.census.gov/compendia/statab/cats/education/higher_education_institutions_and_enrollment.html

# SELECTING A COLLEGE OR UNIVERSITY THAT'S RIGHT FOR YOU

## Worksheet

❑ ***Step 1:*** *Get Started!* Taking the first step is the hardest with any important decision. But after you take that first step, the following steps will be easier. When would you like to start school?

_______________________________________________________________

❑ ***Step 2:*** Decide what your goals are for going to school. Record your goals below.

_______________________________________________________________

_______________________________________________________________

_______________________________________________________________

❑ ***Step 3:*** Understand the options that are available to you.

- ❑ Type of school
- ❑ Type of instructional delivery
- ❑ Accreditation
- ❑ Policy on prior learning assessment
- ❑ Cost
- ❑ General school characteristics

❑ ***Step 4:*** Rate the criteria in order of importance when selecting a school. (3 – highest importance, 1 – lowest importance)

______ Type of school
______ Type of instruction
______ Accreditation
______ Policy on prior learning assessment
______ Cost
______ General school characteristics
______ Other

❏ ***Step 5:*** Develop a list of possible schools and request information from each.

| School | Date Information Requested |
| --- | --- |
| ______________________________ | ______________________________ |
| ______________________________ | ______________________________ |
| ______________________________ | ______________________________ |
| ______________________________ | ______________________________ |

❏ ***Step 6:*** Research, investigate, and research more.

- ❏ Site visit
- ❏ Meet faculty, staff
- ❏ Communicate with alumni
- ❏ Read blogs

❏ ***Step 7:*** Apply to your top choices.

| School | Date Applied |
| --- | --- |
| ______________________________ | ______________________________ |
| ______________________________ | ______________________________ |
| ______________________________ | ______________________________ |
| ______________________________ | ______________________________ |

❏ ***Step 8:*** Select your school! ______________________________

# CHAPTER 7

## Connecting Learning to Earning: Understanding the Big Picture

Selecting and beginning a career should be so simple: *You decide what you want to do; you go get the course work to qualify for the career you want; you apply for and get the job you want.*

As we all know, however, if it were that simple, we wouldn't have a skills gap in the United States today, and you, in all likelihood, wouldn't be reading this book! In this chapter, we will discuss some of the early developments that drive adult learners to re-think their current reality and then, in many cases, to actively seek transitions in their lives, including education. Then we will provide a series of exercises and web links to assist you in developing your career plan and getting full value for your personal learning.

## TURNING POINTS

Whether or not we have been totally aware of all the personal learning that we have done, at some point we all recognize that we have changed over the years. This recognition can range from a casual observation of the characteristics of aging to a more profound understanding of growth and development.

Although turning points involving experiential learning can be more profound than without the exercise of experiential learning, you continuously acquire knowledge through experiential learning as you grow both personally and professionally. When you acknowledge the changes in your life and the personal learning you have accomplished over time, you bring yourself to a turning point. Turning points are most valuable if they initiate the following progression of events:

1. You come to the realization that you have to change; that things cannot go on the way they are. You re-appraise yourself.
2. You gain confidence and a sense of self-worth as you take stock of your personal learning and accomplishments and become aware of the skills, abilities, and values that you have gained over the years.
3. You become a more conscious learner with your increased ability to reflect on your learning, anticipating future turning points and enhancing the aging process with intellectual maturation through continuous and purposeful learning.

Turning points can be triggered by major events in your life, in many cases, difficult events: a lost job, a divorce, a move, or an illness in your family. The key question, though, is *how will you react to a turning point?* Will you fail to grasp it? Will it overwhelm you? Will it be a wrenching experience that leaves you looking at a stranger in the mirror, wondering who you have become? Or, and this is the heart of the matter, can you convert your turning point into a moment of reflection and self-realization that changes the way you see your place in the world, stimulating more learning and augmenting what you already know?

Successful turning points hinge on a realization of self-worth that comes with the recognition of knowledge that has been learned personally over the years. Sometimes the learning exposed at a turning point is personal, involving your behavior, values, and relationships with other people. At other times it is career-based, relating to your knowledge, skills, abilities, and behaviors on the job. Sometimes it is a combination of the two. However it occurs, a turning point represents a strong change in your perception of yourself in the world and a realization of your self-worth.

## SUCCESSFUL TRANSITIONS

Although your personal and experiential learning affects you dramatically, it is often difficult to recognize or remember clearly because it accumulates one small bit at a time. The all-important next steps are to evaluate your learning, harness its value, and use it consciously in your professional and academic development. A successful transition involves actively seeking a change, taking advantage of a self-awareness or a turning point. As we said at the end of the last section, evaluating experiential learning can be done many ways. Reading *Cashing In* will help you get off to a good start. And, while no one can completely eliminate unpredictable events or negative change – health problems, emotional conflict, employment issues, and other similar situations – being aware of shifts in your attitudes, skills, values, and knowledge can promote a more gradual evolution and understanding of developing skills and self-confidence.

The following stories come from people who have taken a portfolio course as a step on their pathway towards the bachelor's degree. They are shining examples of successful transitions driven by the prior learning development and assessment process. Although the stories are different, there is a common element among them. As the famous experiential educator and philosopher John Dewey said, these people "have the precious ability to learn from the experiences they have." Assisted by their portfolio development course, they have made meaning from their personal learning and, in the process, become conscious and continuous learners. This ability to learn consciously is the key to their continuing success.

This is the story of Elaine. Elaine took a turning point and turned it into a new future through re-direction and education.

## Elaine

Elaine of Montpelier, Vermont, was a math teacher before she took time off to raise her two daughters. She had always planned to return to teaching when her kids went to school. However, a confusing turning point stimulated new insights and led Elaine to make a very different decision about her career.

> *For years I had been thinking that when the girls were in school, I would go back to work teaching. That first year, I took a temporary job at a local coin company running their retail store. I was planning to apply for teaching jobs the following fall. I kept telling people I was just doing it for now, until I could get a job in June teaching, because I wasn't growing. I wasn't learning anything. Then they took it all away from me on New Year's Eve.*
>
> *There had been two major layoffs before then so that the writing was on the wall. But I still thought I had a couple of months, if it was their choice. If it was going to be mine, I had until June. I couldn't foresee that my job was going to end in December.*
>
> *I can't identify the feeling that I felt at the time. There was a strange atmosphere because you were making believe you were happy about something when you really weren't. I was really going to miss that money, and it called my bluff about other jobs.*
>
> *I was in a sort of state of shock for three weeks or so. It sounds like a strong statement to make, but I think I was, because, as I look back on it, I couldn't identify what was going on at the time. I was staying home saying, "Isn't this just wonderful, I can spend all day reading." But it was awful, and I couldn't recognize that. After about a month, I identified the anger, which was good. But then, the depression hit, and I thought, "My God, what am I going to do? My kids are in school, and I'm 35 years old, and I've got to get my act together.*
>
> *So I said, "Okay, you can't wait until June anymore. Now, what are you going to do?" Well, I was going to teach because that had always been my pat answer.*
>
> *So, I started to send resumes to different area schools. I started getting replies. That was the thing that threw me into another depression. Because, at that point, I had to make a commitment. Writing the letters was no commitment.*
>
> *I realized that I didn't want to teach anymore. Of course George had been encouraging me, because he'd been listening to me for ten years and here I was applying for all these jobs, so why wouldn't*

*think that? But, I heard him on the phone one day, telling his parents that I was going back to teaching. And, when I heard it like a third party, all of a sudden I said to myself, "Wait a minute. That's not me. I don't think I'm going to do that. No, I'm not going to do that."*

During those ten years at home raising her children, Elaine's life had changed outwardly. But she wasn't aware of a concurrent inner change in her personal aspirations and expectations. They had evolved so slowly and quietly that she continued to carry a clear but outdated image of herself as a teacher when she returned to work. It wasn't until circumstances gave her no alternative that she confronted the changes in herself. Elaine became more aware of her values. She didn't want to teach any longer. That's when she reached her turning point.

Although she had been changing throughout this time, it took Elaine ten years to reach her turning point. Only when she lost her job and confronted her future starkly was she primed to pursue what she really wanted, thus adding to her new self-awareness caused by her turning point.

*I had always been interested in the law. At one point, I had regretted that I hadn't done something in law when I got out of college. I had heard of the school, Woodbury Associates, before. But I kind of just filed it. Every now and then I'd bring it up with people when I still thought I had a choice. But it was just part of something I was faintly considering.*

*I just didn't know what I was going to do. There was an orientation meeting the following Thursday. I thought, "Maybe that's what I need, right now." so, I gave them a call and told them I'd be there. That unlocked something in me. It cemented the decision and my resolve to go. I felt as if I had made a commitment to something that had been in me for a long time. I sat down that day and wrote two letters, one to my in-laws and one to a friend, and I told them I was going to paralegal school.*

As difficult as it was, Elaine seized her turning point and put the learning it generated to work for her. She learned self-awareness and gained insight into her motives and aspirations when she finally confronted the consequences of being laid off. Then she grappled with the powerlessness that comes from as lack of direction and chose a different course for her life.

## Joan

Joan acquired her personal learning gradually, almost not noticing it. It was not in her life plan to become a successful businesswoman in Des Moines. She did not initially study business, finance, or personnel management in school. Her "undergraduate" education was as a secretary, interior decorator, wife, and mother.

*It's a flow from that early point . . . to today. I have taken hundreds of tiny baby steps . . . I changed a great deal, but the change was made up of those tiny baby steps so I didn't notice it while it was happening . . . As a human being with skills, it's the difference between night and day.*

Yet, when Joan "retired" because her husband was doing so well in his law practice, she was in for a surprise.

> *Bill began making more money, so I started working (at the firm) part-time. Then I retired, thinking, "Oh, I've really made it." Yet I knew within three months that I had not and that I needed to have some kind of challenge. I very quickly got involved in special projects, short-term things, not a career by any means, but interesting, different things.*
>
> *I got involved with Planned Parenthood and became very active in that. I went through the chairs and went on the National Board and Executive Committee. I learned a great deal about money in that context. As a housewife, I was handling thirty or forty thousand dollars a year. The local PP budget grew during my time there from a few hundred thousand to a million dollars. It really started making me understand a lot more about money.*
>
> *At that point I was really getting restless. My children were getting older and I had had a taste of something more than taking dictation and typing. I had done some decision-making and it had sort of spoiled me. I remember a particular night, maybe 15 years ago. We had had a dinner party and a lot of the people had gone home. Some of us were philosophizing and someone asked me, "What is the biggest frustration or unhappiness in your life?" You know, nobody had ever asked me that before and I had never thought about it, and my answer just slipped out, "I have no control over my life." After I said it, I began to think about it. It was definitely a turning point in my life when I began to take control.*

Joan went on to found and develop a successful company. And she drew on her experiential learning to meet many of the problems and issues that arose to confront her. But at the heart of her success was being able to recognize the turning point when it came, and then enrolling in a portfolio course to understand the value of the prior and experiential learning she had done. This was one of the key ways that she learned what "tools" she had in her tool box and then, through additional education and experience, continued to deepen her expertise.

She also became a far more active and conscious learner than she had been before. The portfolio course helped her connect her learning and her behavior so that she could understand who she was becoming as well as what she knew.

> *One way I take stock of myself is when someone says something to me about how they perceive me and all of a sudden I think, "Me. They see me that way." And I compare that image to the way that I see myself.*

## Ray

Ray is another successful learner. But he tells his story from the perspective of being on the outside, looking in on the opportunity that college validation of learning can bring. The respect that he has earned from his fellow officers is reflected in his position as head of the Policeman's Association. But as he approaches 40, Ray is less sure what he wants to do with the rest of his life.

*Sometime in the past, I became aware of how much I really didn't know about things, so I began to read in an effort to know. It made me feel more confident and it made me feel as if I could represent the Policeman's Association better. I can speak my mind now. I am not slow-minded, so I could do the battle, but I just did not feel confident about myself. My mind is a collage of information, you know, that I can dig out and use one of these days. It has made me feel more confident dealing with people and that confidence itself has influenced people.*

*My circle of friends includes a guy with a master's degree in history. He is very bright. People wouldn't imagine a policeman with an IQ of 150. He is hiding and he knows it. Maybe I am as well. But I feel . . . it makes me feel good that I can communicate with these (intelligent) people.*

*Eighty percent of the things I know, I learned on the streets. Those things don't fit exactly into an institution of higher learning. But, the biggest thing that a college could do for me is to be able to write on my resume that I had these degrees that I don't have so I would be invited for an interview. I'm not the only one who feels that way, I'm really not.*

*I don't know if I am who I want to become yet. I don't know the answer to that. But, here is what I do know. I know that I am brighter than the average person around. I know that if I can take that intelligence and integrate it into my reading and then take the insight into people that I have gained over all these years that very few people have seen, I probably know more about people than I do about anything else.*

*Honestly, if you could combine those things with all the knowledge I have about how the world really is and some other things I might have going for myself, and my intelligence, then I have a lot of what I need to know, but I don't yet have the degree.*

## COMPLETE THE CONNECTION: LEARNING TO EARNING

As you discover from these learners and their stories, real people dealing with real issues, you can feel the power of their learning, the improved ability to make judgments, and the impact of the learning that came to each of them when they went through the process of reflecting, organizing, and having their prior and experiential learning assessed. And, indeed, each one of these people has been through an assessment process, personally and educationally. They knew that simply recognizing their personal learning on their own would not be enough. Getting formal validation for it is an essential next step.

Whether it comes from an employer or a college, we all can greatly benefit from the validation of our personal learning. But it has not been easy to do this for most adult learners. That's what *Cashing In* is about, creating an awareness of the opportunity to connect your learning to earning. For far too many people, however, achieving success as a personal learner is not sufficient to earn credit in colleges or to get the promotions they deserve in the workplace. In fact, most businesses like practical experience, but they also feel more confident if a college degree is part of the resume.

## Validation of Competencies

The portfolio development and assessment process is a suitable tool to collect and measure competencies. Instead of seat-time or credit hours, some colleges are moving to a competency-based approach; the certificate or degree is earned through the demonstration of knowledge and skills required in a subject area. This unique approach provides the learner an opportunity to

- earn credit for what they have already learned,
- document and provide meaningful documentation of skills and abilities to employers, and
- align needed career skills with coursework.

## Validation of Learning

The validation of your learning through the assessment process has several significant monetary payoffs. First, as mentioned in other chapters, validating the learning through the assessment process has a payoff toward your degree by saving time and money. The savings in time and money can be very substantial, depending on your learning and experience and on the tuition rate at your school. The savings in tuition is tangible and obvious; however, the time factor can propel you to a promotion or to your next job faster – having a potentially even greater financial impact than the tuition savings.

Secondly, the payoff of a degree increases your earning potential. According to the U.S. Bureau of Labor Statistics, those with a bachelor's degree have an average weekly income of $1,066 while those with only a high school diploma have an average weekly income of $652 per week (U.S. Bureau of Labor and Statistics, 2012). With each level of degree, beginning with an associate's degree, the median weekly income level rises. In addition, it's no secret that having a degree gives you a competitive edge when looking for a job or wanting to change jobs.

## Complete the Connection

When turning points emerge, use them to your benefit. You may not capture them all, but even a few successful transitions can be the pivotal point that you need to make that change to *Cash In* on your lifelong learning. Recognizing your personal learning is the first step; go for the validation. Go for the recognition of the knowledge that you've acquired over the years whether personal- or career-based.

# WEB RESOURCES

### Bureau of Labor Statistics

http://www.bls.gov/emp/ep_chart_001.htm

The Bureau of Labor Statistics maintains earnings and unemployment rates by educational attainment.

### CollegeMeasures.org

http://collegemeasures.org/

CollegeMeasures.org focuses on using data and statistics to inform, measure, and understand the performance of schools.

### Competency-Based Degree Programs in the United States

http://www.cael.org/pdfs/2012_CompetencyBasedPrograms

This 2012 CAEL (Council for Adult and Experiential Learning) report describes the history and current state of competency-based degree programs.

### Trends in Higher Education: Education Pays

http://trends.collegeboard.org/education_pays

Last published in 2010 by the College Board, Education Pays reports on the benefits of a college education.

### Qualified

https://qualfied.net

Use this free resource to build a skills profile connected to current job postings. You also have access to courses to thousands of courses.

### Western Governors University

http://www.wgu.edu/why_WGU/competency_based_approach

Western Governors University uses a competency-based to learning. Your degree is earned through the demonstration of skills and knowledge.

## REFERENCES


Smith, P. (1986). *Your Hidden Credentials: the Value of Learning Outside of College.* Acropolis Books, Inc.

U.S. Bureau of Labor Statistics. (2012). Earnings and unemployment rates by educational attainment. Retrieved June 25, 2013 from http://www.bls.gov/emp/ep_chart_001.htm (pp 23-27, 42-47, 62-64).

# CHAPTER 8

## Financing Your Education

Education is an investment. It is an investment of time, energy, and, of course, money. While the payoff over the life of your career can far exceed the upfront expense of the education itself, figuring out how to pay for it in the first place can feel overwhelming. Going to school is a big decision, and working out how to pay for your education is a big part of that decision. As an adult learner, you do have options. Before you make any financial commitments, do your homework to become knowledgeable and informed about the financial commitment and the various options for financing your education.

### WHAT IS THE PRICE OF ATTENDING COLLEGE?

Unfortunately, there is no simple answer to this question. The cost of your education will depend on which school you select, what degree or program you select, and the length of the degree or program. The price can range from thousands to tens of thousands depending on the college and the degree.

It is, however, possible to estimate the cost. Effective October 29, 2011, the Higher Education Act of 2008 requires that each U.S.-based college and university that participates in the Federal Title

IV programs must publish a Net Price Calculator (NPC) that provides estimated prices of attendance, which includes expenses such as tuition and fees, room and board, estimated books and supplies, and grant aid available. Federal Title IV programs include loans, grants, and work-study funded by the federal government. Of course, you do want to make sure that you follow up with each school you are considering seriously for more definitive tuition and fees, but this will provide you with a rough estimate when you are researching which school to attend (Chapter 6).

## DECREASING THE COST OF COLLEGE

The tuition cost of most traditional colleges depends on, among other things, the number of semesters or credits you need to earn the degree and graduate. Thus one of the first things to consider when trying to work out how to pay for college is whether or not you can cut down on the cost by reducing the number of classes you need to take or credits you need to accumulate for graduation. It is no secret that the cost of college continues to rise. But if you have knowledge and skills that can help you earn credit for courses through prior learning assessment (PLA), your total tuition costs will be reduced.

### Low- or No-Cost Courses and Training

In addition to the recognized and accepted methods of PLA described in Chapter 3, there are a number of nontraditional, yet reputable options available that can help you gain college-level knowledge, skills, and credit at a price that is significantly lower than tuition at a traditional college or university.
Organizations are developing and delivering no- or low-cost courses and training aids:

- StraighterLine (www.straighterline.com) is an organization that provides students with access to online college courses for a monthly subscription fee. StraighterLine partners with numerous colleges and universities that accept credit for its courses. StraighterLine's courses also have been approved by the American Council on Education's College Credit Recommendation Service. (See Chapter 3 for more details on ACE CREDIT.)
- Khan Academy (www.khanacademy.org) provides more than 1,800 short, simple video lectures and chalkboard demonstrations covering subjects including math, physics, and economics. Although Khan Academy does not offer credit for courses, it does provide students with knowledge and skills that they can use to earn credit through PLA (see Chapter 3).
- More and more colleges are offering open content. Open courses are just that—free and open to anyone. While they are not college-credit bearing courses, they can help prepare you for, or enhance, your college experience. They may provide you with the learning you need to earn college credit by a standardized test or by a form of PLA. For more information on open courses, check out Open Courseware Consortium for a list of colleges supporting open learning at www.ocwconsortium.org.

## Know Your Finance Options

No matter how you plan to pay for your education, do your homework. Know what you are committing to, know the terms, know the repayment guidelines, and know the limits. Not all financial aid options are created equal.

Also, be aware that tuition isn't the only cost associated with an education. You will also incur course fees, books, and lab fees. If you are attending class, you may also have the additional expense of gas for your car, bus fee, and maybe even the expense of a babysitter. Other costs to consider include your time away from work, missed wages, and other opportunities that you may miss because you need to attend to classes and coursework.

There are a number of ways to pay for your education.

**Cash Pay** If you have the funds, you can pay directly using your own personal resources. However, even if you are able to pay cash for your education, you should still research program-specific grant or scholarship options. Every year, scholarship or grant funding goes unused either because the grantor can't find students meeting the criteria or students simply fail to apply.

**Employer Tuition Benefits** Many employers offer tuition reimbursement as part of an employee benefits package. Ask your Human Resources department about tuition benefits. Even if the tuition benefit does not fully cover your expenses, any free money can reduce your total financial burden.

**U.S. Department of Education's Federal Student Aid** Financial aid from federal programs is the largest source of student aid. More than $50 billion in federal aid is paid out on an annual basis to more than 15 million students. Federal student aid is in the form of grants and loans.

**GI Bill** If you have served in the military, check with the college or university VA (Veteran's Affairs) representative for information and an application for Education benefits. You can also apply for benefits online or call 1-888-Gi BILL-1. You can use the Road Map for Success to help you with deciding which benefit is the best for you.

**Credit or Personal Loan.** Check with your personal bank about an educational loan; most banking institutions have a special rate for educational loans. But before going down that road, submit the Free Application for Federal Student Aid (FAFSA) to see if you qualify for loans subsidized by the federal government. Federal loans have lower interest rates than banks. (See *What is FAFSA* below).

**Credit Card.** Beware of financing any part of your education with a credit card. Credit card rates can be very high and are rarely comparable to educational loan rates. Many students unintentionally finance part of their education with credit cards when they use credit cards for living expenses. It is very important not to rely on your credit card for your basic living expenses. Instead, budget your living expenses, like rent, food, and car insurance, into your loans; the interest rate will be much, much lower.

## Types of Financial Aid

Financial aid is typically determined based on two things, merit and need. Merit-based aid is financial assistance granted based on a student's achievement or potential, and is typically awarded without considering the student's financial need. Merit-based aid usually comes in the form of scholarships or grants that do not have to be paid back. The financial backing of merit-based aid is typically from donors or an outside organization. Each school will have a list of grants or scholarships available, so be sure to ask! Students who do not qualify for need-based assistance (but could, nevertheless, use the assistance) may qualify for merit-based aid. Need-based assistance is calculated based solely on the student's financial situation. Some need-based assistance is in the form of grants that do not need to be paid back, while some is in the form of loans that do need to be paid back.

**Federal Financial Aid** The largest provider of student aid in the United States is the government. Types of federal financial aid include direct loans, grants, and work-study:

- There are two types of federal loans, Perkins and Direct. The Perkins funds are provided to the schools for undergraduate and graduate students with financial need. The schools disburse the funds. There are four types of Direct loans:
  - Subsidized loans are available for undergraduate students that demonstrate a financial need.
  - Unsubsidized loans are available for undergraduate, graduate, and professional students; students do not have to demonstrate a financial need.
  - PLUS loans are available for graduate and professional and to parents of undergraduate students.
  - Consolidated loans are loans available to students to provide the opportunity to combine various federal loans into one.
- The Pell Grant is the largest and most utilized grant provided by Federal Student Aid. Pell Grants are available only to undergraduates, and are based on need, cost of attendance, and enrollment status. Pell Grants do not have to be repaid.
- The Federal Work Study (FWS) program provides funds to schools for part-time student employment. The FWS is based on student need and the availability of work study may vary from school to school.

**School-based Scholarships and Grants** Funds may be available through your college or university. Some are degree- or career-specific, while others are based on need. Check with the school's financial aid office to see what may be available for you. School-based aid differs between schools and comes from donors, corporate partnerships, or federal funds.

**Private Scholarships and Grants** National private or non-profit organizations may provide private scholarship and grants as a way to attract employees, increase visibility of education within their organization, or bring awareness to a cause. For example, you may find scholarships and grants by companies such as AT&T, Comcast, or Boeing to attract interest in their companies. Private scholarships and grants are sometimes competitive; you may have to write an essay or participate in an interview to be eligible. Check with your financial aid office for any private scholarships and grants available. Also, check the website for any company where you have an interest in working for any posted scholarships or grants.

## What Is FAFSA?

FAFSA is the acronym for the Free Application for Federal Student Aid. An office of the US Department of Education, Federal Student Aid (www.fafsa.ed.gov/) is the largest provider of student aid. It is responsible for the management of financial aid programs that come under Title IV of the Higher Education Act of 1965.

Need-based aid is financial assistance that is based on financial need as determined by completing the FAFSA. Need-based aid is calculated based on income and other financial factors, but not on merit. Once you have your prospective list of schools, complete the FAFSA. It is highly likely that whether or not you quality for any federal aid, the school will require that you complete a FAFSA. You can complete the FAFSA online; just be sure to have income, tax, and other financial information handy. When need-based aid is awarded, it may be in the form of grants or scholarships that do not need to be paid back, or in loans that do need to be paid back. Many students finance their education using a combination of grants, scholarships, and loans.

Complete and submit your FAFSA online at www.fafsa.ed.gov. Be sure to review the application requirements as you will need to have your personal financial records available while you are completing the online application. You can begin this process at any time; however, you will not receive the funds until you are admitted and enrolled in a degree program. Although you may not want federal financial aid, many schools require you to apply in order for you to be eligible for any private- or school-related scholarships.

There are eligibility requirements which qualify you for Federal Student Aid. Since there can be changes to the requirements from year to year, you should check the website directly at http://studentaid.ed.gov/eligibility/basic-criteria.

## MAKING FINANCIAL DECISIONS

You have secured financing—*now what*? Figuring out how you're going to pay is just the first step.

### Set an Educational Budget!

Setting a budget will help keep your expenses in check and your loan payments reconciled. You need to actively manage your budget by routinely balancing your financial aid disbursements and your expenses. This will help catch any mistakes and keep you on track of the exact amount that you have borrowed. It will be up to you to be responsible to manage the money wisely so that it will meet all of your educational expenses:

Begin by identifying potential expenses such as

- tuition and fees,
- transportation,
- books and supplies, and
- personal expenses.

- Keep records. Whether you are receiving federal, state, or employer money, keep records of the payments that you receive. Also keep a record of what you are paying out in tuition and expenses in case you quality for a year-end deduction on your taxes.
- Make regular appointments with your financial aid advisor. Working with federal aid can be tricky so stay in touch with your advisor for any updates.
- Remember, if you receive loans, they will need to be repaid. Check on the terms of the loans that you accept so that you understand when repayment will begin.
- Reassess your situation periodically. You may find that you did not need as much aid as you originally thought. In this case you may want to start paying back the loans early. Alternatively, you may find that you need more. Before putting all those extra expenses on a credit card, talk to your financial aid advisor about securing more loans.

## Financial Aid Pitfalls

Be aware of the financial aid pitfalls. Many students end up paying more than they need to for their education either because they miss out of cost-savings opportunities or do not fully understand their financing options and responsibilities. Common pitfalls include

- Not applying for federal aid. Completing and submitting the FAFSA is free; submit your application as it can qualify you for school-based scholarships or grants – the free money!
- Submitting incorrect information on your FAFSA. Submitting incorrect information can cause delays. Corrections will have to be made and your application resubmitted.
- Missing financial aid deadlines. Although the federal deadline may be June 30, often the schools have a much earlier deadline. Check with your financial aid office to make sure you stay on track and don't miss deadlines.
- Borrowing more than you need. Just because you may qualify for a larger amount doesn't mean that you need to take it! You should only borrow what you need. Yes, it is tempting, but remember – it will have to be repaid, and you will be paying interest on that money.
- Missing the opportunity to have your learning assessed for college-level credit. Don't forget about requesting credit for learning you've acquired outside the classroom. This can save you significant time and money toward your degree. See Chapter 3 for more information on PLA and earning credit for non-traditional learning.
- Not scheduling time with your financial aid advisor. Utilize your college resources; they are knowledgeable and can help connect you with local resources and keep you informed about any changing requirements.
- Scams! Yes, there are scams that promise guaranteed results. Remember the saying, "if it's too good to be true, it probably is." Watch out for grand promises. And remember, the FAFSA is free! You shouldn't be charged for a free resource. Don't confuse FAFSA.gov, the official government site, with FAFSA.com, a private company that charges a fee!
- Failure to repay student loans. Repayment is expected with student loans, just like any other consumer loan. Failure to repay will have a negative impact on your credit rating as well as other finance-related issues. When you receive a loan, be sure you fully understand the terms of repayment.

## There's an App for That!

StudentAdvisor, a *Washington Post* company that is part of Kaplan Higher Education Group's Innovation team, developed and released the ScholarshipAdvisor application. ScholarshipAdvisor helps students find scholarships and other forms of financial aid, and also provides free access to updated college reviews. www.studentadvisor.com

## Key Terms

**FAFSA.** The Free Application for Federal Student Aid
**Grant.** A form of financial aid that does not need to be paid back
**Loan.** A form of financial aid that must be paid back
**Merit-based aid.** Financial aid that is awarded based on a student's achievement or potential, not financial need
**Need-based aid.** Financial aid that is awarded solely on the basis of a student's financial need

# WEB RESOURCES

## The price of attending college

### National Center for Education Statistics: Net Price Calculator Requirements

https://nces.ed.gov/ipeds/resource/net_price_calculator.asp

All postsecondary institutions that participate in the Title IV federal student aid programs are required to post a net price calculator on their websites. The calculator provides an estimated net price (tuition and other costs minus scholarships and financial aid) to current and prospective students and their families based on a student's individual circumstances. A net price calculator is required for all Title IV institutions that enroll full-time, first-time degree, or certificate-seeking undergraduate students.

### The College Board's Net Price Calculator

http://studentnpc.collegeboard.org/

The College Board's Net Price Calculator provides you with an estimated cost of participating colleges and universities based on the institution's *sticker price* and your financial circumstances.

### National Center for Education Statistics: Tuition costs of college and universities

http://nces.ed.gov/fastfacts/display.asp?id=76

Follow the trends in the cost of a college education published by the U.S. Department of Education.

## Decreasing the cost

(See more resources to help you decrease the cost by earning credit for prior learning in Chapter 3.)

### Khan Academy

www.khanacademy.org

Khan Academy has thousands of college-level lectures open and available to the public. You can use these to help you learn material to pass exams and develop a portfolio.

### Open Courseware Consortium

www.ocwconsortium.org

The Open Courseware Consortium provides free and open access to college-level courses developed by major educational institutions.

### StraighterLine

www.straighterline.com

Check out StraighterLine for information on courses available for a low monthly fee.

## Applying for financial aid

### Free Application for Federal Student Aid (FAFSA)

www.fafsa.gov

Federal Student Aid, a part of the U.S. Department of Education, is the largest provider of student financial aid in the nation. The FAFSA website allows you to access, complete, and file the federal financial aid application for free. Don't confuse FAFSA.gov with FAFSA.com!

### Department of Education: Federal Student Aid

http://studentaid.ed.gov/home

This site from the U.S. Department of Education includes information on the different types of aid available, who gets aid, how to apply for aid, and how to repay aid.

### U.S. Department of Veterans Affairs

http://www.va.gov/

Find the latest information on educational benefits provided by the Department of Veterans Affairs.

### bigfuture by the College Board

https://bigfuture.collegeboard.org/

Explore multiple tools to help you find colleges, explore careers, or pay for college.

### Student Advisor

http://www.studentadvisor.com/

StudentAdvisor, a *Washington Post* company that is part of Kaplan Higher Education Group's Innovation team, developed and released the ScholarshipAdvisor application. ScholarshipAdvisor helps students find scholarships and other forms of financial aid, and also provides free access to updated college reviews.

## Creating a Budget

### Financial Planning: Budget Worksheet for College Students

http://financialplan.about.com/library/n_collbudget.htm

This template from About.Com will help you create a budget to help manage your expenses and income.

### Microsoft- College budget template

http://office.microsoft.com/en-us/templates/college-budget-TC010336268.aspx

You can download this template from Microsoft into Excel to help you create a budget to help manage your expenses and income.

# CHAPTER 9

## Understanding Transfer Policies

As an adult learner, you have probably attended a college or two at some point. You may have attended simply to gain specific knowledge or skills; or perhaps you started taking classes toward a degree but never finished. If you have attended a higher education institution and earned college credit, you will be considered a transfer student when you return to school. It is important to gather all of your previously earned credits to eliminate duplicating coursework and to reduce the number of courses needed to earn a degree. This chapter will help you understand what transfer means, how the transfer process works and how transfer policies may affect you.

## WHAT IS TRANSFER?

Transfer is the process by which students move their credit earned from one higher education institution to another. Because students are more mobile than ever, they may transfer a number of times before earning a degree. Students have different reasons for transferring between institutions, including job relocation, family obligations, unhappiness with an institution, cost, and degree selection. Many adult learners seek to transfer credits when returning to college after a long hiatus.

There are three types of transfer pathways:

1. **Lateral transfer** is a move between two similar institutions, such as from a two-year to a two-year school.
2. **Vertical transfer** is a move from a lower degree-granting institution to a higher degree-granting institution such as the transfer from a two-year to a four-year college.
3. **Reverse transfer** is a move from a higher degree-granting institution to a lower degree-granting institution such as from a four-year to a two-year school.

The most common transfer path is the two-year to four-year; however the rise in the numbers transferring from four-year to two-year is gaining the attention of educators.

## HOW THE TRANSFER PROCESS WORKS

The definition is much simpler than the process itself. Credit transfer is the movement of college credit earned at one institution to be recognized and accepted at another institution, known as the receiving institution. For example, let's say you attended a community college in Georgia for your undergraduate program, but you didn't have an opportunity to complete it before you move to another state. A few years later, you enroll in a college in Florida to finish your degree. You don't want to start all over. You want to have your new college in Florida recognize the courses that you previously took, so you request a transcript of your completed courses be sent to your new school. Your new school in Florida will review your transcript from your school in Georgia as *transfer* credit.

The acceptance of transfer credit is not guaranteed. Because similar courses can be taken at multiple schools with different policies, different curricula, and different program levels, the process to transfer credit can be very uncertain and confusing. Added to the confusion is the fact that there is no single, uniform model for the transfer of credit between institutions in the United States. For the most part, unless you are covered under an articulation agreement or common course numbering (described below), there is no guarantee that any particular course you take will be transferable. The decision regarding the transfer of credit is determined solely by the *receiving* institution.

The U.S. Department of Education has created some online tools to improve transparency within higher education and to provide students with institutional information. These tools include the College Navigator, the Financial Aid Shopping Sheet, and the College Scorecard (see the Web Resources at the end of this chapter). Use these sites that you can use to research and to compare transfer processes and information about schools. (Note that these tools are still fairly new and their data-collection methods and analytics are still being updated.)

### Other Forms of Transfer

States are becoming increasingly creative with their efforts to attract and retain students. As a result, students have improved access to transfer credit and greater mobility between schools. Some of these efforts involve developing articulation agreements and common course numbering.

**Articulation Agreement** An articulation agreement is a pre-defined agreement between one or more institutions outlining the academic criteria and process for students to transfer college-level coursework between institutions. Courses included in the articulation agreement are very specific and defined, but their transferability is guaranteed. Articulation agreements are prevalent in certain fields, career pathways, and trades. For example, a four-year institution may have articulation agreements with local career or technical schools to provide a continued path for learners that would like to continue their education. You can also refer to your state department of education website for existing state articulations, which define institutions and courses that transfer between schools in the same state.

**Common Course Numbering** The common course numbering system involves applying a single identification number and prefix to courses in different institutions that cover the same core content and have the same learning outcomes. The common course numbering system is typically adopted and agreed upon by a group of schools within the same state. For example, in Florida, *BSC 005* is General Biology. This course covers basically the same content whether you take it at Everglades University or Florida Gulf Coast University. Using the same course identification number across institutions enables students, faculty, and administrators to easily recognize the courses. It also makes it easier to transfer credit between schools within the same state system.

## Tips for Transfer Students

As the traditional student has evolved to become more non-traditional, the pattern of transfer and mobility of students is also changing. It is no longer uncommon for a student to transfer between one and three times before earning a degree. A 2012 report, "Transfer and Mobility: A National View of Pre-Degree Student Movement in Postsecondary Institution," (National Student Clearinghouse Research Center) examined the complexity of transfer patterns over a five-year period. The five main observations from the report were

- One-third of all students transferred at least once within five years.
- The most prevalent transfer destination was public two-year institution.
- The most common time of the first transfer was in the student's second year.
- Transfer rates were similar for part- and full-time students.
- Over one-quarter of all transfers crossed state lines.

Given this high frequency of student transfer, and the varied reasons for transfer, it is important to consider the transferability of your current course credits even if you have no intention to transfer. Make sure the classes you are taking now are likely to transfer later, should you need them to.

# PLANNING A TRANSFER

As with any event, planning for a transfer will provide a smoother experience. And as with other big decisions, there are a few guidelines to consider when considering a transfer to another school:

1. First, check out the general policies for transfer students at your college or university. Each institution has its own policies and processes for handling transfer students. Use the transfer school's resources, and speak to an enrollment advisor about your transfer.
2. Not all classes may be eligible for transfer, which could have an impact your degree progress or your pace for graduation. Ask specific questions about your courses and how they will transfer.
3. Ask about the maximum number of credits your intuition or program will accept. In many cases, there are very clear policies on the number of credits that can be transferred into an institution.
4. Clarify the transferability of older courses. If there may have been substantial changes to the curriculum or knowledge base, as in many technology- and health-related fields, your credits are unlikely to transfer.

## Understanding How Credit Transfer Policies May Vary

Each school may have its own credit transfer program, so you should be prepared to encounter various guidelines when attempting to transfer credit. Here are some of the policies you may encounter.

**Maximum Credits Transferred** Typically, institutions will establish a limit to the number of credits that can be transferred from other institutions. The policy regarding the maximum number of credits transferred will differ with each institution. The maximum number allowable for transfer can also depend on the program.

**Residency Requirements** An academic residency requirement refers to the minimum number of credits required to be completed at an institution to earn a degree from that institution. The residency requirement will differ with not only the institution, but also the program.

**Prior Learning Assessment** The prior learning assessment category may simply be called the "other" category. *Other* includes credit earned by non-traditional means such as credit by exam, ACE-reviewed military, or corporate training. Different colleges have different policies about what they will accept in terms of credits for prior learning.

**Accreditation** Transferability has everything to do with accreditation: an institution's transfer policy will specify what is required in terms of the accreditation status of the university or program where the course was taken. In many cases, regionally accredited institutions will only accept transfer credit from other regionally accredited institutions.

**Grade Standards** Most schools' transfer policies specify a minimum grade that you must have earned in the course order for credit to be transferable.

## SUMMARY

While it is not necessary to know the ins-and-outs of transfer policies intimately, you should understand how they may possibly affect you. You may begin your education at one institution without any plans to transfer, but life happens. Ask the questions up front to know whether you are spending your time and money on a program that is transferrable. If you are a transfer student, then it's more important than ever to do your research and ask questions to ensure that you are able to maximize your transfer. There is nothing more frustrating for an adult learner to get months or years into a degree program to find out that it not transferrable or recognized by another institution, or that he or she wasted time retaking courses for credit that could have been transferred from a previous institution. Be prepared: Do your research, understand the process of transfer, be knowledgeable about the questions you need to ask, and plan your transfer.

### Key Terms

**Accreditation.** The process by which an independent organization (an accrediting agency) assesses an educational institution or program to determine whether or not it meets educational standards.

**Articulation Agreement.** An articulation agreement is a partnership between two or more schools to ensure a smooth transfer of credits from institution to institution. The agreement specifies student and institution requirements for the transfer of credits.

**Common Course Numbering.** A system of numbering college courses in a standardized way such that they are easily recognized between institutions usually within the same state.

**Credit Transfer.** Credit transfer is the procedure by which college credit earned at one institution is recognized and accepted by another institution. Transfer credit is not guaranteed until it is reviewed, accepted, and posted to your official record at your receiving institution.

**Transfer Credit.** Transfer credit is course credit that has been earned at one institution and then transferred to another to count toward a degree.

## WEB RESOURCES

**Understanding the Transfer Process**
http://media.collegeboard.com/digitalServices/pdf/advocacy/policycenter/understanding-transfer-process-community-college-ihep-121217.pdf

This report by the Institute for Higher Education Policy (IHEP) will help you understand the transfer policy, as well as trends and characteristics of transfer students.

**Recurring Trends and Persistent Themes: A Brief History of Transfer**
http://media.collegeboard.com/digitalServices/pdf/advocacy/policycenter/recurring-trends-persistent-themes-history-transfer-brief.pdf
This article from the College Board provides a historical analysis of trends and influence on transfer policies.

**State Higher Education Policy Database**
http://higheredpolicies.wiche.edu/content/policy/state/summaries/31
Western Interstate Commission for Higher Education's (WICHE) State Higher Education Policy Database provides state and national policymakers, education leaders, practitioners, and education consumers with an inventory of state-level policies and resources in key policy issue areas related to student achievement, access, and success in higher education.

## REFERENCES

National Student Clearinghouse Research Center. (2012). *Transfer and Mobility: A National View of Pre-Degree Student Movement in Postsecondary Institution*. Herndon, VA. http://pas.indiana.edu/pdf/Transfer%20&%20Mobility.pdf

# GLOSSARY

**Accreditation or accreditation processes** The process by which an independent organization (an accrediting agency) assesses an educational institution or program to determine whether or not it meets educational standards. The goal of accreditation is to ensure that education provided by higher education institutions meets acceptable levels of quality.

**Accredited institution or accredited program** An educational institution such as a college or university, or a degree or certification program, that meets a set of standards, as assessed by an independent, private organization (an accrediting agency).

**Accrediting Agency** (or accreditation agency) Accrediting agencies are private educational associations of regional or national scope that set standards for delivering high quality education, and that assess educational institutions and programs to determine whether or not the institutions and programs meet those standards.

**Articulation agreement** An articulation agreement is a partnership between two or more schools to ensure a smooth transfer of credits from institution to institution. The agreement specifies student and institution requirements for the transfer of credits.

**Bloom's Taxonomy** Bloom's Taxonomy is a hierarchical classification system of thinking and learning that is use used in the development of learning statements that are included in a learner's Course Petitions. In Bloom's taxonomy, thinking and learning activities are classified according to cognitive level, from lower-level *knowledge, comprehension,* and *application*, to higher level *analysis, synthesis*, and *evaluation*. Learning statements that are built around higher levels of Bloom's taxonomy are viewed as representing higher quality, more rigorous learning than those built around lower levels.

**CLEP** CLEP stands for *College Level Examination Program*, which is a national program that provides standardized examinations in a number of subjects, allowing learners to earn college credit for their learning (see The College Board – www.collegeboard.com).

**Certification** A certification represents a level of knowledge or skills attainment, as recognized officially by a certification-granting institution.

**Challenge exams** Challenge exams are developed by institutions for a specific program and are designed to give adult learners credit for knowledge acquired outside the institution.

**Common Course Numbering** A system of numbering college courses in a standardized way such that they are easily recognized between institutions usually within the same state.

**College-level Learning** Learning that meets the course outcomes or course objectives for a course offered by an accredited postsecondary higher education institution.

**Core Course** A core course is a fundamental course of a particular degree program. Which courses are considered to be core courses depends on the school and degree focus and generally include the courses required in a specific program or degree. For example, for a business degree, the core courses may include principles of business, business math, or introduction of marketing.

**Course Outcomes** Course outcomes are specific learning goals that describe the focus of a course and what learners will be able to do or understand after successfully completing the course.

**Course Petition** As part of an experiential learning portfolio, a course petition is a document that shows how experiential learning maps to specific college-level courses.

**Credit Recommendation** In prior learning assessment (PLA), credit recommendation is an assessment provided by one or more subject matter experts that indicates whether the learner should be awarded college credit for his or her experiential learning, based on established criteria. An evaluator provides recommendations credit based on the student's documentation and demonstration of whether college-level learning has occurred and whether all of the course outcomes for a given course have been met.

**Credit Transfer** Credit transfer is the procedure by which college credit earned at one institution is recognized and accepted by another institution. Transfer credit is not guaranteed until it is reviewed, accepted, and posted to your official record at your receiving institution.

**Degree audit** The degree audit is an analysis of a student's progress toward a degree. A degree audit provides a student a picture of his or her progress in a degree program, and identifies unfulfilled requirements. A degree audit is a tool typically used in academic planning.

**Educational Goal Statement** An educational goal statement outlines the goals of a learner, and is one of the components of a portfolio or other evidence presented for assessment toward credit. The intent of a goal statement is to help a person in the PLA process clarify his or her short- and long-term educational, personal, and/or professional goals in order to set a context for the assessment process.

**Electives** Also known as general electives, open electives, or free electives, electives are a group of courses within a degree program that are not specifically required for the degree. In contrast to "requirements" or "required courses," electives are typically open for the learner to select based on their interest.

**Expanded Resume** Part of an experiential learning portfolio, an expanded resume is a detailed list of work and life experience from which a learner has acquired knowledge, skills, and abilities. An expanded resume includes sections on employment history, education and technical skills, professional activities, and extracurricular activities.

**Experiential Learning** Experiential learning is learning involves direct participation or observation and results in the acquisition of knowledge, skills, and abilities. Often, experiential learning is gained outside the traditional college classroom, through work and life experiences.

**General education course** Depending on the school you attend, general education (often abbreviated "gen ed") courses are typically common to all degree programs and include subjects such as English composition, math, science, history, government, and arts.

**Grant** A grant is a form of financial aid that does not need to be paid back.

**Hybrid course** Often called a blended course, a hybrid course is a mixture of multiple formats such as online and face-to-face or self-paced and online.

**Learning Autobiography** As part of an experiential learning portfolio, a learning autobiography is a chronological, first-person narrative that describes what an individual has learned from experience and how their learning has grown.

**Major** The major is the subject- or discipline-focus of a program or degree. The word can be used as a noun: One can have a major in mathematics, sociology, business, and so on. It can also be used as a verb: One can major in one of a large number of subjects. Each institution has regulations that determine how many courses must be completed in one's major subject area to fulfill the requirements of the degree.

**Merit-based aid** Merit-based aid is financial aid awarded based on the student's achievements or potential, not on financial need.

**Minor** The minor is a secondary subject- or discipline- focus of a program or degree. This is the secondary subject or academic department outside of the major in which a student takes concentrated coursework. A minor generally consists of four or more courses in one area of study.

**MOOC** A MOOC is a Massive Open Online Course. MOOCs are free and open to the public. Knowledge and skills gained from a MOOC can be used toward portfolio development or to help pass an exam, either of which an adult can then use to earn college credit.

**Need-based aid** Need-based aid is financial aid awarded based solely on the student's financial need.

**Non-traditional Learning** Non-traditional learning is typically any learning acquired outside a formal classroom setting, such as on the job training, professional development, or trainings for certification.

**OpenCourseWare (OCW)** OpenCourseWare (OCW) are free and open digital publications of high quality university-level educational materials. These materials are organized as courses, and many include course planning materials and evaluation tools as well as thematic content.

**Portfolio** In prior learning assessment (PLA), a portfolio is a collection of evidence that supports a learner's claim for credit. It is a formal communication presented by the learner as part of a petition requesting credit or recognition for learning outside of the classroom setting. The portfolio must make its case by identifying learning clearly and succinctly, and it must provide sufficient evidence (information and documentation) so that evaluators can use it as the basis for their review. The portfolio is the package used in recommending, and potentially awarding, college credit for learning.

**Prior Learning Assessment (PLA)** PLA is a term used by colleges and universities to describe the process of earning college credit for learning that is acquired through a learner's work and life experiences, outside the traditional college classroom. The goal of PLA is to help adult learners earn college credit for what they already know, and achieve their educational goals more quickly and less expensively.

**Receiving Institution** During credit transfer, the receiving institution is the college that credit is being transferred to.

**Transfer Credit** Transfer credit is course credit that has been earned at one institution and then transferred to another to count toward a degree.

**Validated Learning** Validated learning is learning that has been reviewed by a college, university, or a third party assessor of college-level learning. Learning from courses taken at a college or university or demonstrated on standardized examinations, along with other evaluated learning (perhaps by the American Council on Education), are examples of validated learning.

www.ingramcontent.com/pod-product-compliance
Ingram Content Group UK Ltd.
Pitfield, Milton Keynes, MK11 3LW, UK
UKHW051331130926
15127UKWH00013B/100

9 781465 241993